THE CAÑONS OF THE COLORADO

BY MAJOR JOHN WESLEY POWELL
With Illustrations by Thomas Moran and Others

EDITOR'S PREFACE

THE Colorado River Exploring Expedition is what John Wesley Powell called his collection of 9 men, 4 boats, 10 months' rations, personal gear, tools, and scientific instruments as he began charting the last major unexplored region of the then United States on May 24, 1869.

The Expedition's boats had been built in Chicago, their limited funding had come from Illinois natural history and state educational sources, their rations had been provided through a joint resolution of the Congress by the U.S. Army, their instruments had come from the Smithsonian Institution, transportation expenses for both men and boats had been waived by the railroads, and personal expenses were borne individually by the members. No well-funded government survey this, sponsored by an energetic young nation eager to locate its natural treasures. No, it was a group of mountain men looking for adventure, and who thought they would find it with Powell. And find it they did!

After starting in the river at Green River, Wyoming, the party had expected to overwinter somewhere along the way, but the loss of rations, boats, and the desertion of 4 of the men

"EMMA DEAN" IN MARBLE CANYON.

TAU-GU, A CHIEF OF THE PAIUTE INDIAN TRIBE AND MAJOR POWELL IN SOUTHERN UTAH.

changed those plans, and so they pushed on through the labyrinthic depths of Utah, Colorado, and Arizona to reach the mouth of the Virgin River in Nevada and Mormon pioneers there on August 30, 1869, just over 3 months later. Their feat was a remarkable one. Often they had to commit their fate to the river's whims, not knowing what lay ahead around the bend of the rapid, for noone had yet even traversed the area by land — that is why they were on the river, as it offered the only even potentially feasible route through the region! Frequently they were wrecked and had to stop to make their own repairs.

Powell, of course, was motivated by science as well as a love to travel and explore in making this 1869 journey — and another like it in 1871.

He not only recorded his observations of the geology and stream courses of the main river but made excursions up side canyons and onto the cliffs. He also noted ancient Indian ruins and studied those then living in the area.

Powell was 35 years old when he made this first trip, a professor of natural history and curator for universities and museums in Illinois. He had already seen service in the Civil War as a volunteer from Illinois, and it was during the Battle of Shiloh that he had lost his right arm, a fact to be remembered as you read his almost-nonchalant statements of river-running in a small boat and of his cliff-climbing exploits.

Later, Powell was to become the first director of the U.S. Geological Survey and to make scientific contributions in the fields of ethnography and in studies of the arid lands. One of his official recommendations, had it been followed, could well have avoided or at least diminished the effect of the Dust Bowl droughts of the 1930s and subsequent emigration from that area.

The present account we reprint here was prepared by Powell as a popular presentation of his river-running discoveries; it was first printed in 1875 in *Scribner's Monthly,* a national journal of that early day. Its form was as three articles, or papers, which ran serially. Two additional articles describing an overland trip to the Grand Canyon and the pueblo Indian villages of the plateau country were produced just following. (These are also available through the present publisher, address below).

Withal, these early materials give a colorful, scientific, and now-historic description of the country — and are so fascinating as to have produced the broadest interest nationally for over a century. But to further enhance their appeal, the fine illustrations of the early American landscape painter Thomas Moran have been added, plus others as well. The Moran artwork was produced as a result of a later trip Moran made into the country (but not down the river) with Powell; many of these illustrations accompanied the original 1875 *Scribner's Monthly* articles; others have been added from Powell's more scientific *Exploration of the Colorado River,* also 1875. We are further indebted to the U.S. Geological Survey and to the Denver Western History Library for additional illustrations and assistance, and to the National Park Service staff at Grand Canyon National Park for their aid, too.

Powell's trip can no longer be made. There can be only one first. Besides, immense dams now block the canyons and reservoir waters (one is called Lake Powell) now flood their former winding courses. But stretches of the near-wild river can still be run, and thousands yearly make such trips today through scenic reaches of the river still preserved in national park areas like Dinosaur, Canyonlands, and Grand Canyon. River-running thus has an enduring quality just for fun as well as personal discovery, but with some reading of early accounts like this one of Powell, you can also relive history in vicarious fashion and, through increased understanding, heighten your enjoyment still more.

William R. Jones

John Wesley Powell's Pioneer River Voyage-1869

EXPLANATION

1. Green River (Wyo.)
2. Flaming Gorge
3. Lodore Canyon
4. Split Mountain Canyon
5. Ouray
6. Desolation Canyon
7. Gray Canyon
8. Green River (Utah)
9. Labyrinth Canyon
10. Catacract Canyon
11. Hite
12. Glen Canyon
13. Crossing of the Fathers
14. Lee's Ferry
15. Marble Canyon
16. Bright Angel
17. Kaibab Plateau
18. Grand Canyon
19. Separation Canyon
20. St. George

VOYAGE BEGAN MAY 24, 1869

VOYAGE ENDED AUGUST 30, 1869

Relief map of Powell's pioneer river voyage—1869.

after U.S. Geological Survey

CLIFFS OF GREEN RIVER.

by Thomas Moran

by Thomas Moran

THE START FROM GREEN RIVER STATION.

THE CAÑONS OF THE COLORADO.

BY MAJOR J. W. POWELL.
in three papers
I. DOWN THE GREEN RIVER.

THE Colorado River is formed by the junction of the Grand and the Green. Grand River has its source in the Rocky Mountains, five or six miles west of Long's Peak, in latitude 40° 17′ and longitude 105° 40, approximately. A group of little Alpine lakes that receive their waters from perpetual snow banks discharge into a common reservoir known as Grand Lake—a beautiful sheet of water, whose quiet surface reflects towering cliffs and crags of granite on its eastern shore, and stately pines and firs on its western margin.

Green River heads near Fremont's Peak in the Wind River Mountains. This river, like the last, has its sources in Alpine lakes fed by everlasting snows. Thousands of these little lakes with deep, cold, emerald waters, are embosomed among the crags of the Rocky Mountains. These streams, born in the gloomy solitudes of the upper mountain region, have a strange and eventful history as they pass down through gorges tumbling in cascades and cataracts until they reach the hot, arid plains of the lower Colorado, where the waters that were so clear above, empty muddy floods into the Gulf of California.

Green River is larger than the Grand, and is the proper continuation of the Colorado. Including this river, the whole length of the stream is about two thousand miles. The region of country drained by the Colorado and its tributaries is about eight hundred miles in length, and varies from three hundred to five hundred in width, containing about three hundred thousand square miles, —an area larger than all of New England and the Middle States, with Maryland and Virginia added.

There are two distinct portions of the basin of the Colorado. The upper two-thirds of the basin rises from four to eight hundred feet above the level of the sea. This higher region is set on the east, north and west, with ranges of snow-clad mountains attaining an altitude above the sea, varying from eight thousand to fourteen thousand feet.

The lower third is but little above the level of the sea, but here and there ranges of eruptive mountains rise to an altitude of from two to six thousand feet. This part of the valley is bounded on the north by a line of cliffs which forms a bold, often vertical step, hundreds or thousands of feet to the table-lands above.

Very little water falls within the basin, but, all winter long, snows fall on its mountain-crested rim, filling the gorges, half burying the forests, and covering the crags and peaks with a mantle woven by the winds from the waves of the sea. When the summer sun comes, these snows melt and tumble down the mountain-sides in millions of cascades. Ten million cascade brooks unite to form ten thousand torrent creeks; ten thousand torrent creeks unite to form a hundred rivers beset with cataracts; a hundred roaring rivers unite to form the Colorado, which rolls a mad, turbid stream into the Gulf of California.

Consider the action of one of these streams, its source in the mountains where the snows fall, its course through the arid plains. Now, if at the river's flood storms were falling on the plains, the channel of the stream would be cut but little faster than the adjacent country would be washed, and the general level would thus be preserved; but, under the conditions here mentioned, the river deepens its bed, as there is much erosion, and but little lateral degradation. So all of these streams cut deeper and still deeper year by year, until their banks are towering

INDIAN LODGE IN THE UINTA VALLEY

cliffs of solid rock. These deep, narrow gorges are called cañons. For more than a thousand miles along its course the Colorado has cut for itself such cañons. The Rio Virgen, Kanab, Paria, Escalante, Dirty Devil, San Rafael, Price and Uinta, on the west; the Grand, Yampa, San Juan, and Little Colorado on the east—have also cut for themselves such narrow, winding gorges or deep cañons. Every river entering these has cut another cañon; every lateral creek has cut a cañon; every brook runs in a cañon; every rill born of a shower, and born again of a shower, and living only during these showers, has cut for itself a cañon; so that the whole upper portion of the basin of the Colorado is traversed by a labyrinth of these deep gorges.

About the basin are mountains; within the basin are cañon gorges; the stretches of land from cañon brink to cañon brink are of naked rock or drifting sands, with here and there lines of volcanic cones, and with black scoria and ashes scattered about. These cañon gorges and desert wastes have prevented the traveler from penetrating the country, so that, until the Colorado River Exploring Expedition was organized, it was almost unknown; yet, enough had been seen to foment rumor, and many wonderful stories have been told in the hunter's cabin and explorer's camp. Stories were related of parties having entered the gorge in boats and having been carried down with fearful velocity into whirlpools, where all were overwhelmed in the abyss of waters; others of underground passages for the great river into which boats had passed, never to be seen again. It was currently believed that the river was lost under the rocks for several hundred miles. There were other accounts of great falls whose roaring music could be heard on the distant mountain summits. There were stories current of parties wandering on the brink of the cañon vainly endeavoring to reach the stream below, and perishing with thirst at last, in sight and sound of its tantalizing waters.

The Indians, too, have woven the mysteries of the cañons into the myths of their religion. Long ago there was a great and wise chief who mourned the death of his wife and would not be comforted until Tahvwoats, one of the Indian gods, came to him and told him that she was in a happier land, and offered to take him there that he might see for himself, if, upon his return, he would cease to mourn. The great chief promised. Then Tah-vwoats made a trail through the mountains that lie between that beautiful land, the balmy region in the Great West, and this, the desert home of the poor Nu-ma. This trail was the cañon gorge of the Colorado. Through it he led him; and when they had returned, the deity exacted from the chief a promise that he would tell no one of the joys of that land, lest, through discontent with the circumstances of this world, the people should desire to go to Heaven. Then he rolled a river into the gorge, a raging stream that should engulf any who might attempt to enter thereby. More than once have I been warned by the Indians not to enter this cañon; they considered it disobedience to the gods and contempt for their authority, and believed that it would surely bring their wrath upon me.

For two years previous to the exploration I had been making some geological studies among the heads of the cañons running into the Colorado from the east, and a desire to explore the Grand Cañon itself grew upon me. Early in the spring of 1869 a small party was organized for this enterprise. Boats were built in Chicago and transported by rail to the point where the Union Pacific Railroad crosses Green River. With these we were to descend the Green into the Colorado, and the Colorado down to the foot of the Grand Cañon.

On the 24th of May the good people of Green River City turned out to see us start. We raised our little flag, pushed the boats from shore, and the swift current carried us down.

Our boats were four in number—three built of oak, stanch and strong, double-ribbed, with double stern and stern-posts, and further strengthened by bulk-heads, dividing each into three compartments. Two of these, the fore and aft, were decked, forming water-tight cabins. The little vessels were twenty-one feet long, and were capable of carrying about four thousand pounds each, and, without the cargoes, could be transported by four men. The fourth boat was made of pine, very light, but sixteen feet in length, with a sharp cut-water, and every way built for fast rowing, and divided into compartments as the others.

We took with us rations deemed sufficient to last ten months, expecting to stop over for the winter at some point about midway down the stream. We also took tools for repairing boats and building cabins. For scientific work we had sextants, chronometers, barometers, thermometers, compasses, and other instruments.

The flour was divided into three equal parts, the meat and other articles of our rations, in the same way. Each of the larger boats had an axe, hammer, saw, auger, and other tools, so that all were loaded alike.

We distributed the cargoes in this way, that we might not be entirely destitute of some important article should any one of the boats be lost. In the small boat we packed a part of the scientific instruments, three guns, and three small bundles of clothing, only. In this boat I proceeded in advance to explore the channel.

J. C. Sumner and William H. Dunn were my boatmen in the "Emma Dean." Then followed "Kitty Clyde's Sister," manned by W. H. Powell and G. Y. Bradley. Next, the "No Name," with O. G. Howland, Seneca Howland, and Frank Goodman; and last came the "Maid of the Cañon," with W. R. Hawkins and Andrew Hall.

Sumner was a soldier during the late war, and before and since that time has been a great traveler in the wilds of the Mississippi Valley and the Rocky Mountains as an amateur hunter. He was a fair-haired, delicate-looking man, but a veteran in experience, and had performed the feat of crossing the Rocky Mountains in midwinter on snow-shoes. He spent the winter of 1866-7 in Middle Park, Colorado, for the purpose of making some natural history collections for me, and succeeded in killing three grizzlies, two mountain lions, and a large number of elk, deer, sheep, wolves, beavers, and many other animals. When Bayard Taylor traveled through the parks of Colorado, Sumner was his guide, and he speaks in glowing terms of Mr. Taylor's genial qualities in camp, but he was mortally offended when the great traveler requested him to act as door-keeper at Breckenridge to receive the admission fees from those who attended his lectures.

Dunn had been a hunter, trapper, and mule-packer in Colorado for many years. He dressed in buckskin with a dark oleaginous luster, doubtless due to the fact that he had lived on fat venison and killed many beavers since he first donned his uniform years ago. His raven hair fell down to his back, for he had a sublime contempt for shears and razors.

Captain Powell was an officer of artillery during the late war and was captured on the 22d day of July, 1864, at Atlanta, and served a ten months' term in prison at Charleston, where he was placed with other officers under fire. He was silent, moody, and sarcastic, though sometimes he enlivened the camp at night with a song. He was never surprised at anything, his coolness never deserted him, and he would choke the belching throat of a volcano if he thought the spitfire meant anything but fun. We called him "Old Shady."

Bradley, a lieutenant during the late war, and since orderly-sergeant in the regular army, was, a few weeks previous to our start, discharged, by order of the Secretary of War, that he might go on this trip. He was scrupulously careful, and a little mishap worked him into a passion, but when labor was needed, he had a ready hand and powerful arm, and in danger, rapid judgment and unerring skill. A great difficulty or peril changed the petulant spirit into a brave, generous soul.

O. G. Howland was a printer by trade, editor by profession, and hunter by choice. When busily employed he usually put his cap in his pocket, and his thin hair and long beard streamed in the wind, giving him a wild look, much like that of King Lear in an illustrated copy of Shakespeare which tumbled around the camp.

Seneca Howland was a quiet, pensive young man, and a great favorite with all.

Goodman was a stranger to us—a stout, willing Englishman, with florid face, and more florid anticipations of a glorious trip.

Billy Hawkins, the cook, was a soldier in the Union army during the war, and, when discharged at its close, went West, and since then had been engaged as teamster on the plains or hunter in the mountains. He was an athlete and a jovial good fellow, who hardly seemed to know his own strength.

Hall was a Scotch boy, nineteen years old, with what seemed to us a "second-hand head," which doubtless came down to him from some knight who wore it during the Border Wars. It looked a very old head indeed, with deep-set blue eyes and beaked nose. Young as he was, Hall had had experience in hunting, trapping, and fighting Indians, and he made the most of it, for he could tell a good story, and was never encumbered by unnecessary scruples in giving to his narratives those embellishments which help to make a story complete. He was always ready for work or play, and was a good hand at either.

Our boats were heavily loaded, and only with the utmost care was it possible to float on the rough river without shipping water. Our way for nearly fifty miles was through the Green River Bad Lands, a region of desolation. The rocks are sandstones and shales, gray and buff, red and brown, blue and black strata in many alternations, lying nearly horizontal, and almost without soil or vegetation; but they are all very soft and friable, and are strangely carved by the rains and streams. The fantastic rain-sculpture imitates architectural forms, and suggests rude and weird statuary. Standing on some high point, you can look off in every direction over a vast landscape, with salient rocks and cliffs glittering in the evening sun. At such a time dark shadows are settling in the valleys and gulches, and the heights are made higher, and the depths deeper, by the glamour and witchery of light and shade. Away to the south the Uinta Mountains stretch in a long line—high peaks piercing the sky, and snow fields glittering like lakes of molten silver, and pine forests in somber green, and rosy clouds playing around the borders of huge black masses; and heights and depths, and clouds and mountains, and snow fields, and forests, and rocklands are blended into one grand view.

The journey to the foot of the mountains was made with no more important incident than the breaking of an oar in some ugly rapid, or the killing of a mountain sheep on a cliff that overhangs the river.

The general course of the Green here is to the south. The Uinta Mountains have an east and west direction, and stand directly athwart the course of the stream; yet it glides along quietly as if a mountain range were no formidable obstruction to its progress. It enters the range by a flaring, brilliant red gorge, that may be seen from the north-west a score of miles away. The great mass of the mountain ridge through which the gorge is cut is composed of bright vermilion rocks, but they are surmounted by broad bands of mottled buff and gray, and these bands come down with a gentle curve to the water's edge on the nearer slope. This is the head of the first cañon which we were to explore, an introductory one to a series made by the river through this range. We named it "Flaming Gorge." The cliffs or walls on either side we found to be about twelve hundred feet high.

You must not think of this mountain range as a line of peaks standing on a plain, but as a broad platform many miles wide, from which the mountains have been carved by the waters. You must conceive, too, that this plateau is cut by gulches and cañons in many directions, and that beautiful valleys are scattered about at various altitudes. The first series of cañons we explored constitutes a river-channel through such a range of mountains. The cañon is cut nearly half way through the range, then turns to the east, and is cut along the central line or axis, gradually crossing it to the south. Keeping this direction for nearly fifty miles, it then turns abruptly into a south-west course, and goes diagonally through the southern slope of the range. Here and there the walls are broken by lateral cañons, the channels of little streams entering the river. Where the river has the general easterly course above mentioned, the western part only runs in a cañon, while the eastern half of its course is through a broad valley called, in honor of an old-time trapper, "Brown's Park," and long known as a favorite winter resort for mountain men and Indians.

On the 30th of May we started down the mysterious cañons, with some anxiety. The old mountaineers had told us it could not be run; we had heard the Indians say: "Water heap catch 'em!" But all were eager for the trial. Entering Flaming Gorge, we quickly ran through it on a swift current, and emerged into a little park. Half a mile below, the river wheeled sharply to the left, and we turned into another cañon cut into the mountain. We entered the narrow passage; on either side the walls rapidly increased in altitude; on the left were overhanging ledges and cliffs five hundred, a thousand, fifteen hundred feet high; on the right the rocks were broken and ragged; the water filled the channel from cliff to cliff. Then the river turned abruptly around a point to the right, and the water plunged swiftly down among the great rocks. And here we had our first experience with cañon rapids. I stood up on the deck of my boat to seek a way between the wave-beaten rocks. All untried as we were with such waters, the moments were filled with intense anxiety. Soon our boats reached the swift current; a stroke or two, now on this side, now on that, and we threaded the narrow passage with exhilarating velocity, mounting the high waves whose foaming crests dashed over us, and plunging into the troughs until we reached the quiet water below. And then came a feeling of great relief; our first rapid was run. Another mile and we came out into the valley again.

The course of this cañon is remarkable. Where the river turns to the left, above, it penetrates the mountain to its very heart, then wheels back upon itself, and runs out into the valley from which it started, but half a mile below the point at which it entered, so that the cañon is in the shape of an elongated letter U, with the apex in the center of the mountain.

Soon we left the valley and entered another short cañon, very narrow at first, but widening below as the walls increased in altitude. The river was broad, deep, and quiet, and its waters mirrored towering rocks. Kingfishers were playing about the stream, and so we adopted as the name, "Kingfisher Cañon."

At the foot of this cañon the river turned to the east, past a point which was rounded of eighteen hundred or two thousand feet. Each step of this amphitheater was built of red sandstone, with a face of naked, red rock and glacis clothed with verdure; so that the amphitheater was surrounded by bands of red and green. The evening sun lit up the rocks and the cedars, and its many-colored beams danced on the waves of the river. The landscape reveled in sunshine.

Below Bee-Hive Point we came to dangerous rapids, where we toiled along for some days, making portage or letting our

INQUIRING THE WAY.

to the shape of a dome; on its sides little cells had been carved by the action of the water, and in these pits, which cover the face of the dome, hundreds of swallows had built their nests; and as they flitted about the rock they looked like swarms of bees, giving to the whole the appearance of a colossal bee-hive, of the old-time form; and so we named it "Bee-Hive Point."

One evening when we camped near this point, I went out into a vast amphitheater, rising in a succession of terraces to a height boats down the stream with lines. Now and then we had an exciting ride; the river rolled down at a wonderful rate, and where there were no rocks in the way, we made almost railroad speed. Here and there the water rushed into a narrow gorge, the rocks on the sides rolled it into the center in great waves, and the boats went bounding over these like things of life. Sometimes the waves would break and their waters roll over the boats, which made much bailing necessary, and obliged us to stop occasionally for that purpose. At one time we made a run of twelve miles in an hour, including stoppages.

The spring before, I had a conversation with an old Indian, who told me about one of his tribe attempting to run this cañon: "The rocks," he said, holding his hands above his head, his arms vertical, and looking between them to the heavens, "the rocks h-e-a-p, h-e-a-p high; the water go h-oo-woogh, h-oo-woogh; water-pony (boat) h-e-a-p buck; water catch 'em! no see 'em Injun any more! no see 'em squaw any more! no see 'em pappoose any more!" Those who have seen these wild Indian ponies rearing alternately before and behind, or "bucking," as it is called in the vernacular, will appreciate his description.

One day we came to calm water, but a threatening roar was heard in the distance below. Slowly approaching the point from which the sound issued, we came near the falls and tied up just above them on the left. Here we were compelled to make a portage; so we unloaded the boats, fastened a long line to the bow, and one to the stern of the little boat, and moored her close to the brink of the fall. Then the bow-line was taken below and made fast, the stern-line was held by five or six men, and the boat let down as long as they could hold her against the rushing waters; then, letting go one end of the line, it ran through the ring, the boat leaped over the fall, and was caught by the lower rope. In this way the boats were passed beyond the fall. Then we built a trail among the rocks, along which we carried our stores, rations and clothing, and the portage was completed after a day's labor. On a high rock, by which our trail passed, we found the inscription: "Ashley 18–5;" the third figure was obscure, some of the party reading the date 1835, some 1855.

James Baker, an old-time mountaineer, once told me about a party of men starting down the river, and Ashley was named as one of them. The story runs that the boat was swamped and some of the party drowned in one of the cañons below.

The word "Ashley" was a warning to us,

and we resolved on great caution. We named the cataract "Ashley Falls." The river is very narrow at that point, the right wall vertical for two or three hundred feet,

by Thomas Moran

THE CAMP AT FLAMING GORGE.

and the left towering to a great height with a vast pile of broken rock lying between the foot of the cliff and the water. Some of the rocks broken from the ledge above have tumbled into the channel and caused this fall. One great cubical block, thirty or forty feet high, stands in the middle of the stream, and the waters, parting to either side, plunge down about twelve feet and are broken again by smaller rocks into a rapid below. Immediately below the falls the water occupies the entire channel, there being no talus at the foot of the cliffs.

Near the foot of this cañon there is a little park, which is simply the widening of the cañon into a little valley; this we called "Red Cañon Park." Reaching this on the third of June, we spread our rations, clothing, etc., on the ground to dry, and several of the party went out for a hunt. I took a walk of five or six miles up to a pine-grove park, its grassy carpet bedecked with crimson flowers set in groups on the stems of pear-shaped cactus plants; patches of painted cup were seen here and there with yellow blossoms protruding through scarlet

The next day we ran down to Brown's Park and found a quiet river through this valley until we reached the Gate of Lodore, the entrance to the Cañon of Lodore.

On the 7th of June three of us climbed to the summit of the cliff on the left and found its altitude above camp to be 2,086 feet. The rocks are split with fissures, deep

THE GATE OF LODORE.   by Thomas Moran

bracts; little blue-eyed flowers were peeping through the grass, and the air was filled with fragrance from the white blossoms of a spiræa; a mountain brook ran through the midst, ponded below by beaver dams. This quiet place formed a great contrast to the one I had just left.

and narrow, sometimes a hundred feet or more to the bottom. Lofty pines find root in such fissures as are filled with loose earth and decayed vegetation. On a rock we found a pool of clear cold water caught from a shower which had fallen the evening before. After drinking of this we walked to the brink of the cañon and looked down to the water below. The cañon walls are buttressed on a grand scale, and deep alcoves are excavated; rocky crags crown the cliffs, and the river rolls below. At noon we returned to camp. The sun shone in splendor on the vermilion walls, shaded into green and gray where the rocks were lichened over; the river filled the channel from wall to wall, and the cañon opened like a beautiful door-way to a region of glory. But at evening, when the sun was going down and the shadows were setting in the cañon, the vermilion gleams and roseate hues, blended with tints of green and gray, slowly changed to somber brown above, and black shadows crept over them below. Then it seemed the shadowy portal to a region of gloom. Through this gate-way we were to enter on our voyage the next day.

Entering the cañon, we found, until noon, a succession of rapids, over which our boats had to be taken by lines. Here I must explain our method of proceeding at such places. The "Emma Dean" went in advance, and the other boats followed in obedience to signals. When we approached a rapid, or what on other rivers would be called a fall, I stood on deck to examine it while the oarsmen "backed water," and we drifted on as slowly as possible. If I could see a clear chute between the rocks, away we went; but if the channel was beset entirely across, we signaled the other boats to pull to land, and I walked along the shore for closer examination. If this revealed no clear channel, our hard work began; we dropped the boats to the very head of the dangerous place, and let them over by lines or made a portage; frequently carrying both cargoes and boats over the rocks, or perhaps only the cargoes, if it was safe to let the boats down. The waves caused by such a river differ much from the waves of the sea. The water of an ocean wave merely rises and falls, the form only passes on, and form chases form unceasingly. A body floating on such waves merely rises and sinks—does not progress unless impelled by the wind or some other power; but here the water of the wave passes on, while the form remains. The waters plunge down ten or twelve feet at the foot of a fall, then spring up again in a great wave, then down and up, down and up, in a series of billows that gradually disappear in the more quiet stream below. But these waves are always there, and you can stand above and count them. A boat riding such waves leaps and

plunges along with great velocity. Now, the difficulty in riding over these falls, when the rocks are out of the way, is in the first wave at the foot. This will gather sometimes for a moment, heaping up higher and higher until it breaks back. If the boat strikes it the instant after it breaks, she cuts through it, and the breaker dashes its spray over the boat, and would wash us overboard did we not cling tight. If the boat, in going over the falls, chances to get caught in some side current, and is turned from its course so as to strike the wave "broadside on" and the wave breaks over us in the same instant, the boat is capsized. Still we must cling to her, for she cannot sink, the water-tight compartments acting as buoys. And so we go, dragged through the waves until still water is reached. We then right the boat and climb aboard. We had several such experiences that day. And so, from day to day, we toiled on through the Cañon of Lodore.

One night we were camped on the right bank, on a little shelving rock between the river and the foot of the cliff. With night comes gloom into these great depths. After supper we sat by our fire made of drift-wood caught by the rocks, and told stories of wild life. It was late before we spread our blankets on the beach. Lying down, we looked up through the cañon and saw that only a little of the blue heaven appeared overhead—a crescent of blue sky with but two or three constellations peering down upon us. I did not sleep for some time, as the excitement of the day had not worn off. Soon I saw a bright star that appeared to rest on the very verge of the cliffs overhead on the east. Slowly it seemed to float from its resting-place on the rocks over the cañon. At first it appeared like a jewel set on the brink of the cliff, but as it moved out from the rock I almost wondered that it did not fall. In fact it did seem to descend in a gentle curve, as though the bright sky, in which the stars were set, was spread across the cañon, resting on either wall, and swayed down by its own weight. The star appeared to be in the cañon, so high were the walls. I soon discovered that it was the bright star Vega, so it occurred to us to designate that part of the wall as "The Cliff of the Harp."

Very slowly we made our way through this cañon, often climbing on the rocks at the edge of the water for a few hundred yards, to examine the channel before running it. One afternoon we came to a place where it was necessary to make a portage.

WINNIE'S GROTTO, SIDE CANON OF LODORE.

suddenly narrowed by rocks which have tumbled down from the cliffs, or have been washed in by lateral streams. Immediately above the narrow rocky channel on one or both sides, there is often a bay of quiet water, in which it was easy to land. Sometimes the water descends with a smooth, unruffled surface from the broad, quiet spread above, into the narrow, angry channel below, by a semicircular sag. Great care was taken not to pass over the brink into this deceptive pit, but above it we could row with safety. At this point I walked along the bank to examine the ground, leaving one of the men with a flag to guide the other boats to the landing place. I soon saw one of the boats make shore all right, and felt no more concerned; but a minute after, I heard a shout, and, looking around, saw one of the boats shoot down the center of the sag. It was the "No Name," with Captain Howland, his brother, Seneca Howland, and Frank Goodman. I felt that its going over was inevitable, and ran to save the third boat. A few minutes more and she turned the point and headed for the shore. Then I started down stream and scrambled along to look for the boat that had gone over. The first fall was not great, only ten or twelve feet, and we often had run such; but below, the river tumbled down again for forty or fifty feet in a channel filled with dangerous rocks that broke the waves into whirlpools and beat them into foam. I passed around a great crag just in time to see the boat strike a rock, and, rebounding from the shock, careen and fill the open compartment with water. Two of the men lost their oars. Then she swung around and was carried down at a rapid rate, broadside on, for a few yards, and, striking amidships on another rock with great force, was broken quite in two, and the men were thrown into the river. The larger part of the boat still floated buoyantly; this they soon seized, and drifted down the river past the rocks for a few hundred yards to a second rapid filled with huge bowlders. Here the boat struck again, was dashed to pieces, and the men and fragments were carried beyond my sight. Running along, I turned a bend and saw a man's head above the water, dashed about by the waves in a whirlpool below a great rock. It was Frank Goodman clinging to the rock for his life. Then I saw Howland trying to go to his aid from an island on which he had been washed. Soon he came near enough to reach Frank with a pole, which he ex-

The little boat was landed, and the others signaled to come up. Where these rapids, or broken falls, occur, usually the channel is

tended toward him. The latter let go the rock, grasped the pole, and was pulled ashore. Seneca Howland was washed farther down the island, and was caught by some rocks, and, though somewhat bruised, managed to get ashore in safety.

And now the three men were on an island with a swift, dangerous river on either side and a fall below. The "Emma Dean" was soon brought down, and Sumner, starting above, as far as possible, pushed out. Right skillfully he plied his oars, and a few strokes set him on the island at the proper point. Then they all pulled the boat up stream, until they stood in water up to their necks. One sat on a rock and held the boat until the others were ready to pull, then he gave the boat a push, clung to it with his hands and climbed in as they pulled for the mainland, which they reached in safety. We were as glad to shake hands with them as if they had returned from a voyage around the world, and had been wrecked on a distant coast. We named the scene of this incident "Disaster Falls."

The next day, making a portage in the remaining boats, we discovered, a little below, some fragments of an old boat, an old dutch bake-oven, some tin plates and other articles, doubtless the relics of Ashley's party, whom I have before mentioned. The story runs that some of his companions were drowned — how many, I have now forgotten; but Ashley himself and one other survived the wreck, climbed the cañon wall and found their way across the Wasatch Mountains to Salt Lake, liv-

ing chiefly on berries, as they wandered through an unknown and rugged country. When they arrived at Salt Lake, they were almost destitute of clothing and nearly starved. The Mormon people gave them food and clothing and employed them to work on the foundation of the Temple until they had earned sufficient to enable them to leave the country. Of their subsequent history I have no knowledge. It is possible that they returned to the scene of the disaster, as a little creek entering below

THE WRECK AT "DISASTER FALLS."   by Thomas Moran

the cañon is known as Ashley's Fork, and it is reported that he built a cabin and trapped on this stream for one or two winters; but this may have been before the disaster.

Below, we found rocks, rapids, falls, and made our portages. At many places the Cañon of Lodore has deep, dark alcoves set between massive buttresses. In these alcoves grow beautiful mosses and delicate ferns, while springs burst out from the farther recesses and wind in silver threads over floors of sand. At one place we found three

she was set free, a wave turned her broadside down the stream, with the stem, to which the line was attached, from shore and a little up. They hauled in the line to bring the boat in, but the power of the current, striking obliquely against her, shot her out into the middle of the stream. The men had their hands burned by the friction of the passing line as the boat broke away and sped with great velocity down the

FIRE IN CAMP.

cataracts in quick succession where we were compelled to make three difficult portages, and we named the place "Triplet Falls."

In many places we made portages of our rations and let the boats down with lines. This we found to be no easy task, for where such a body of water, rolling down an inclined plane, is broken into eddies and cross-currents by rocks projecting from the cliffs and piles of bowlders in the channel, it requires excessive labor and much care to prevent the little vessels from being dashed against the rocks or breaking away. Sometimes we were compelled to hold the boat against a rock above a chute until a second line attached to the stem was carried to some point below, and, when all was ready, the first line was detached and the boat given to the current. Then she would shoot down and the men below would swing her into some eddy. One day at such a place we were letting down the last boat, and, as

stream. We gave up "The Maid of the Cañon" as lost; but she drifted some distance and swung into an eddy, in which she spun about until we arrived with the small boat and rescued her.

At one place we had to make a portage of more than half a mile past a wild confusion of waves and rocks, which we called "Hell's Half Mile."

One day we stopped for a late dinner at the mouth of a brook on the right. This little stream comes down from a distant mountain in a deep side cañon. We set out to explore it, but were soon cut off from farther progress up the gorge by a high rock over which the brook ran in a smooth sheet; the rock was not quite vertical, and the water did not plunge over in a fall. Then we climbed up to the left for an hour, until we were a thousand feet above the river, and six hundred above the brook. Just before us the cañon divided, one little stream coming down on the right and another on the left, and we could look away up either of these cañons through an ascending vista to cliffs, and crags, and towers, a mile back, and two thousand feet overhead.

To the right were a dozen gleaming cascades; pines and firs stood on the rocks, and aspens overhung the brooks. The rocks below were red and brown set in deep shadows, but above they were buff and vermilion. The light above, made more brilliant by the bright-tinted rocks, and the shadows below, made more gloomy by the somber hues of the brown walls, increased the apparent depth of the cañons, and it seemed a long way up to the world of sunshine and open sky, and a long way down to the cañon floor. Never before had I received such an impression of the vast height of these cañon walls; not even at the Cliff of the Harp, when the very heavens seemed to rest on their summits.

Late the same afternoon we made a short run to the mouth of another little brook coming down from the left into an alcove filled with luxuriant vegetation. Here camp was made with a group of cedars on one side, and a dense mass of box-elders and dead willows on the other. I went out to explore the alcove, and while away a whirlwind came on, scattering the fire among the dead willows and cedar spray. Soon there was a conflagration. The men rushed for the boats, leaving behind all that they could not readily seize at the instant, and even then they had their clothing burned and hair singed, and Bradley had his ears scorched. The cook filled his arms with the mess-kit, and jumping into a boat stumbled and fell, and away went our cooking utensils into the river. Our plates were gone, our spoons were gone, our knives and forks were gone. "Water catch 'em; h-e-a-p catch 'em!" When on the boats, the men were compelled to cut loose, as the flames, running out on the overhanging willows, scorched them. Loose on the stream they must go down, for the water was too swift to make headway against it, and just below was a rapid filled with rocks. On they drifted, no channel explored, no signal to guide them. Just at this juncture I chanced to see them, but had not discovered the fire, and the strange movements of the men filled me with astonishment. Down the rocks I clambered and ran to the bank. When I arrived they had landed. Then we all went back to the late camp to see if anything left behind could be saved. Some of the clothing and bedding that had been taken out of the boats, a few tin cups, a basin and a camp kettle, were all that was left.

THE RESCUE.

The next day we ran down to the mouth of the Yampa River. The journey from the Gate of Lodore was marked by disasters and toils. At the junction of the Yampa and Green we found a beautiful park, inclosed on every side by towering walls of gray sandstone, smooth and vertical. There are three river entrances into this park—one down the Green, one down the Yampa, and one up the Green; there is a fourth entrance by a side cañon that comes in from the south. Elsewhere this park is unapproachable. The way through the Cañon of Lodore is a difficult and dangerous one. The course of the Yampa for forty miles above its mouth is through another cañon; it also is difficult and dangerous. Green River runs through a cañon below Echo Park, beset with rocks and interrupted by falls. So it may be said that the park has but one practicable entrance, that by a side cañon so narrow in many places that a horseman could scarcely ride through it; yet we found a trail down this side cañon, and evidences that the Indians had camped in this beautiful park; in fact, it had been described to me the year before. The park itself is a beautiful natural garden, with grasses and flowering plants, shrubs, and trees—just large enough for a farm.

Here we encamped for two or three days, for the purpose of repairing boats, drying rations, and to make the observations necessary to determine the latitude and longitude of the junction of the two rivers.

Opposite our camp the wall was high and vertical. The river running to the south for a mile and a-half, turns back upon itself, and the two stretches of river, the first south, the second north, are separated by a wall in many places but ten to twenty feet wide and eight hundred feet high, and, on the east, everywhere vertical or overhanging. I wished to climb this wall for the purpose of measuring its altitude, so one day Bradley and I took the little boat and pulled up stream as far as possible, in order to reach a place where the wall was so broken that it seemed practicable to climb it. We landed on a little talus of rocks at the foot of the wall, but found that we must go still farther up the river; so we scrambled on until we reached a place where the river sweeps against the wall. Here we found a shelf along which we could pass, and then were ready for the climb. We started up a gulch, then passed to the left, on a bench along the wall; then up again, over broken rocks; then we reached more benches, along which we worked until we found more broken rocks and crevices; by which we climbed still up, until we had ascended six or eight hundred feet. Here we were met by a sheer precipice.

Looking about, we found a place where it seemed possible to climb. I went ahead,

Bradley handed the barometer to me, and followed; so we proceeded stage by stage until we were nearly to the summit. Here, by making a spring, I gained a foothold in a little crevice and grasped an angle of the rock overhead. I found I could get up no

by Thomas Moran

ECHO PARK.

farther, and could not step back, for I dared not let go with my hand, and could not reach foothold below without; so I called to Bradley for help. He found a way by which he could get to the top of the rock over my head, but could not reach me. He looked around for some stick or limb of a tree, but found none. Then he suggested that he had better help me with the barometer case, but I feared I could not hold on to it. The moment was critical. I was standing on my toes, and my muscles began to tremble. It was sixty or eighty feet to the foot of the precipice. If I lost my hold I should fall to the bottom, and then perhaps roll over the bench and still farther down the cliff. At that instant it occurred to Bradley to take off his drawers, which he did, and swung them down to me. I hugged close to the rock, let go with my hand, seized the dangling legs, and, with his assistance, was enabled to gain the top.

Then we walked out on a peninsular rock, made the necessary observations for determining its altitude above camp, and returned, finding an easy way down.

On the 21st of June we left Echo Park; our boats floated along the long peninsular rock until we turned abruptly to the southwest and entered another cañon. The walls were high and vertical, the cañon narrow, and the river filled the whole space below, so that there was no landing-place at the foot of the cliff.

The Green is greatly increased by the Yampa, and we now had a much larger river. All this volume of water, confined as it was in a narrow channel, and rushing with great velocity, was set eddying and spinning into whirlpools by projecting rocks and short curves, and the waters waltzed their way through the cañon. The cañon was much narrower than any we had seen. With difficulty we managed our boats. They spun about from side to side; we knew not where we were going, and found it impossible to keep them headed down the stream. At first this caused us great alarm, but we soon found there was but little danger, and that we really were making progress on our way. It was the merry mood of the river to dance through this deep, dark gorge, and right gayly did we join in the sport. But our revel was interrupted by a cataract. We succeeded in landing against the wall, and after three or four hours' labor passed the difficult point.

In like manner, spinning in eddies, making portages, and riding with exciting velocity along portions of the river where the fall was great but the rocks were few, we made our way through Whirlpool Cañon, and camped, on the 23d of June, on an island in a beautiful little park.

The next day Bradley and I started early to climb the mountain to the east; we found its summit to be nearly three thousand feet above camp, and it required some labor to scale it; but from its top—what a view! The walls were set with crags, and peaks, and buttressed towers, and overhanging domes. Turning to the right, the park was below us, with its island groves reflected by the deep, quiet waters. Rich meadows stretched out on either hand to the verge of a sloping plain that came down from the distant mountains. In strange contrast to the meadows are the plains of blue and lilac-colored, buff and pink, brown and vermilion rocks, with all these colors clear and bright. A dozen little streams (dry during the greater part of the year) ran down through the half circle of exposed formations, radiating from the island center to the rim of the basin. Each creek had its system of side streams, and each side stream its system of laterals, and again these were divided so that this outstretched slope of rock was elaborately embossed. Beds of different colored formations ran in parallel bands on either side; the perspective, modified by the undulations, gave the bands a waved appearance and the high colors gleamed in the midday sun with the luster of satin. We were tempted to call this " Ribbon Park."

Away beyond these beds were the Uinta and Wasatch Mountains with their pine forests and snow fields, and naked peaks.

Then we turned to the right and looked up Whirlpool Cañon, a deep gorge with a river in the bottom—a gloomy chasm where mad waves roared; but at that distance and altitude the river was but a rippling brook, and the chasm a narrow cleft. The top of the mountain on which we stood was a broad grassy table, and a herd of deer was feeding in the distance. Walking over to the southeast, we looked down into the valley of White River, and beyond that saw the far distant Rocky Mountains in mellow haze, through which came the glint of snow fields.

On the morning of the 25th of June we entered Split Mountain Cañon, and camped that night near the mouth of a cave at the foot of a great rapid. The waves of the rapid dashed in nearly to the farther end of the cave. We could pass along a little shelf at the side until we reached the back part. Swallows had built their nests in the ceiling, and they wheeled in, chattering and scolding at our intrusion, but their clamor was almost drowned by the noise of the waters. Looking out of the cave, we could see far up the river, with a line of crags standing sentinel on either side, and Mt. Hawkins in the distance.

The next day we ran out of Split Mountain Cañon. At the lower end of this gorge the water was very swift, and we ran with great speed wheeling around a rock now and then with a timely stroke or two of the oars. At one point the river turned from left to right in a direction at right angles to the cañon in a long chute and rolled up and struck the right wall where its waters were heaped up in great billows that tumbled back in breakers. We glided into this chute before we could see the danger, and it was too late to stop. Two or three hard strokes were given on the right, and we paused for a moment, expecting to be dashed against the rock; the bow of the boat leaped high on a great wave; the rebounding waters hurled us back, and the peril was past. The next moment the other boats were hurriedly signaled to land on the left. Accomplishing this, the men walked along the shore, holding the boats near the bank and letting them drift around. We started again and the river soon debouched into a beautiful valley. Gliding down its length for ten miles, we camped under a grand old cotton-wood.

Our way then for several days was on a gently flowing river beset with many islands. Groves were seen on either side—natural

Fourth of July. Here we parted company with Frank Goodman, one of the men who was on the "No Name" when she was wrecked.

Moving down the river on the 7th of June, we left the valley country and entered the Cañon of Desolation. At first its waters were quiet, and the walls were low, but the cut

SWALLOW CAVE.   by Thomas Moran

meadows, where herds of antelope were feeding. Here and there we had views of the distant mountains on the right.

We stopped two or three days at the mouth of the Uinta, and some of us went up the river to the Uinta Indian Agency, forty miles to the north-west, and spent the

edges of the rock were often found to be vertical, sometimes terraced, and in many places the steps of the terraces were sloping. In these great curves vast amphitheaters were formed, now in vertical rocks, now in steps. The salient of rock within the curve is usually broken down in a steep slope, and we stopped occasionally to climb out at such a place. Steadily, too, the walls increased in altitude, and, after a run of a day or two, the waters became more rapid. At last we were in a cañon with ragged, broken walls, with many lateral gulches or cañons entering on either side; the river became rough, and occasionally it was necessary to use lines in passing rocky places.

One day in running a rapid we broke an oar and lost another, and finding no timber in the immediate vicinity, of which new oars could be made, we ran on, hoping to be more successful soon, either in finding drift-wood or discovering some place where we could climb out to the summit of the plateau, which, we could see, was covered with a forest of pines. So our little pioneer boat, the "Emma Dean," was running with but one pair of oars. In this way we came near a rapid. Standing on the boat it seemed to me that we could run it, but coming nearer we found it was dangerous; but we were in waters so swift that, with one pair of oars, we could not reach shore. Vainly Sumner pulled with all his power; still down we drifted. Seeing that running the fall was inevitable, I shouted to Sumner to turn bow down, and signaled the other boats to land. The next moment we shot by a big rock; a reflex wave rolled over our little boat and filled her, another wave tossed the boat over, and I was thrown some distance into the water. I soon found that swimming was very easy, and that I could not sink; it was only necessary to ply strokes sufficient to keep my head above water, but now and then a breaker rolled over me, when I closed my mouth and was carried through it. The boat was drifting ahead of me twenty or thirty feet, and when the great waves were passed I overtook her and found Sumner and Dunn clinging to her. As soon as we reached quiet water we all swam to one side and turned her over; in doing this, Dunn

lost his hold and went under; when he came up, he was caught by Sumner and pulled to the boat. In the meantime we had drifted down stream some distance, and saw another

SUMNER'S AMPHITHEATER.

by Thomas Moran

rapid below. How bad it might be we could not tell, so we swam toward shore, pulling our boat along with all the vigor possible. But we were carried down much faster than we gained upon the shore. At last we reached a huge pile of drift-wood. Our rolls of blankets, two guns and a barometer were in the open compartment of the boat when she went over, and these were thrown out; the guns and barometer were lost, but I succeeded in catching one of the rolls of blankets as it drifted by when we were swimming to shore; the other two were lost. A huge fire was built on the bank, our clothing spread to dry, and then from the drift logs we selected one from which we could make new oars, and the remainder of the day was spent in sawing them out.

But I may not stop to tell all our adventures and mishaps—of rapids and falls, of dangerous rocks, of towering walls, and of wild, magnificent scenery. I may not describe the climb to the summit of the plateau, our hunt among the forests, nor tell about the meadow-bordered lakes above. At last we left the Cañon of Desolation and entered Gray Cañon.

Through this gorge the river is swift, and there were many rapids; when they were comparatively smooth I stood on deck, keeping careful watch ahead, and we glided along, mile after mile, plying strokes now on the right, then on the left, just sufficient to guide our boats past the rocks into smooth water, until we emerged from the cañon below.

The plateau through which Gray Cañon is cut terminates abruptly on the south in a bold escarpment known as the Book Cliffs. The river below the cliffs runs, for a time, through a valley. Extensive sand plains reach back from the immediate river valley as far as we could see, on either side. These naked, drifting sands gleamed brilliantly in the midday sun of July. The heat reflected from the glaring surface produced a curious motion of the atmosphere; little currents were made, and the whole seemed shifting and unstable. One moment, as we looked out over the landscape, the atmosphere seemed to be trembling and moving about, giving the impression of an unstable land; plains, and hills and cliffs, and distant mountains seemed vaguely to be floating about in a trembling, wave-rocked sea, and patches of landscape would seem to float away and be lost, and then reappear. Just opposite our camp there were buttes, composed of rock, that were outliers of cliffs to the left. Below,

they were composed of shales and marls of light blue and slate colors, and above, the rocks were buff and gray and then red. The buttes are buttressed below where the azure rocks were seen, and terraced above through the buff and gray and red beds. A long line of cliffs, or rock escarpment, separates the table-lands through which Gray Cañon is

REPAIRING BOATS AT GUNNISON'S BUTTE, GRAY CANYON.

cut, from the lower plain. The eye can trace these azure beds and cliffs on either side of the river in a long line extending across its course until they fade away in the perspective. These cliffs are many miles in length, and hundreds of feet in height, and all these buttes, great mountain masses of rock, seen through the shifting atmosphere, seem dancing and softly moving about.

(Second Paper.)

After passing the mouth of the San Rafael, we entered the mouth of another cañon. The walls of this were of orange-colored sandstone, very homogeneous, usually vertical, though not very high at first. Where the river swept around a curve, a vast hollow dome might be seen, with many caves and deep alcoves. The river sweeps in great curves and doubles upon itself many times. Sometimes we went by a great bend for several miles and came back within a stone's throw of points where we had been before. We called this "Labyrinth Cañon."

There was an exquisite charm in our ride down this beautiful gorge; it gradually grew deeper with every mile we traveled; the walls were symmetrically curved, grandly arched, and of a beautiful color. They were reflected in the quiet water in many places so as to almost deceive the eye. We were all in fine spirits, and the badinage of the men was echoed from wall to wall. Now and then a whistle, a shout, or the report of a pistol would reverberate among the cliffs,

TOOM-PIN WOO-NEAR TOO-WEAP.   by Thomas Moran
(BUTTES OF THE CROSS)

and the cañon seemed filled with strange weird voices.

Labyrinth Cañon ends abruptly, as did the Cañon of Desolation and Gray Cañon, as the table or great geographical bench through which it is cut terminates on the south in a line of cliffs.

Let us understand these cañons. Leaving the Uinta Valley and going south by land, you climb gradually as you advance, so that on passing to the south a distance of forty miles, you are more than three thousand feet above the starting-point. The country then drops off suddenly by a bold, abrupt step of more than three thousand feet, which in many places is vertical for hundreds of feet. Through this inclined plateau the Cañon of Desolation is cut. To the north, of course, the walls are low; at the southern extremity of the plateau, they are more than three thousand feet high.

Through such another inclined terrace Gray Cañon is cut, except that it is narrower and lower, the azure cliffs which terminate this terrace being but two thousand feet high.

The Orange Cliffs, forming the southern escarpment of the great plateau through which Labyrinth Cañon is cut, are but thirteen hundred feet high. Thus there are three benches, or terraced steps, the escarpments or lines of cliffs, and three great cañons, forming the channel of the river across this terraced land. The northern escarpment we called the Brown Cliffs; the middle, the Book Cliffs; and the southern, the Orange Cliffs.

Climb the cliffs at the foot of Labyrinth Cañon and look over the plain below, and you see vast numbers of sharp, angular buttes, and pinnacles, and towers, and standing rocks, scattered about over scores of miles, and every butte, and pinnacle, and tower so regular and beautiful, that you can hardly cast aside the belief that they are works of Titanic art. It seems as if a thousand battles had been fought on the plains below, and on every field the giant heroes had built a monument, compared with which the pillar on Bunker Hill is but a milestone. But no human hand has placed a block in all those wonderful structures; the rain-drops of unreckoned ages have cut them from the solid rock.

from distant mountain summits and make their homes upon the trees. Grouse feed on the pine-nuts, and birds and beasts have a home from which they rarely wander to the desert lands below. Among the buttes

GLEN CAÑON.   by Thomas Moran

Climb the Book Cliffs, and look off to the south over plains of orange and golden sands, and here and there you see massive towering buttes of gypsum. Sometimes the faces of these buttes are as white as the heart of the alabaster from which they are carved, while in others they are stained and mottled red and brown. These alabaster buttes are in the distance; nearer the foot of the cliffs are buttes of azure shades, capped with massive sandstones and limestones.

The summit of the high plateau, through which the Cañon of Desolation is cut, is fretted into pine-clad hills with nestling valleys and meadow-bordered lakes, for now we are in that upper region where the clouds yield their moisture to the soil. In these meadows herds of deer carry aloft with pride their branching antlers, and sweep the country with their sharp outlook, or test the air with their delicate nostrils for the faintest evidence of an approaching Indian hunter. Huge elk, with heads bowed by the weight of ragged horns, feed among the pines, or trot with headlong speed through the undergrowth, frightened at the report of the red man's rifle. Eagles sail down

on the lower terraces rattlesnakes crawl, lizards glide over the rocks, tarantulas stagger about, and red ants build their playhouse mountains. Sometimes rabbits are seen, and wolves prowl in their quest. But the desert has no bird of sweet song, and no beast of noble mien.

Immediately on leaving Labyrinth Cañon, we entered another with quiet water, so we called it "Still-water Cañon." This cañon is cut through the region of standing rocks which I have before mentioned. The Indians call this "Toom-pin Woo-near Tooweap," the Land of Standing Rocks. It is a weird, grand region. The landscape everywhere away from the river is of rock, a pavement of rock with cliffs of rock, tables of rock, plateaus of rock, terraces of rock, crags of rock, buttes of rock, ten thousand strangely carved forms; rocks everywhere, and no vegetation, no soil, no sand. In long gentle curves the river winds about these rocks.

When speaking of them, we must not conceive of piles of bowlders or heaps of fragments, but a whole landscape of naked rock with giant forms carved on it, cathedral-shaped buttes towering hundreds or thousands of feet, cliffs that cannot be scaled, and cañon walls that make the river shrink into insignificance, with vast hollow domes and tall pinnacles, and shafts set on

Name" and by various mishaps, together with the amount now thrown away, left us but little more than two months' supplies, and to make them last this long we must be fortunate enough to lose no more.

Light-House Rock in the Cañon of Desolation.

On the 19th of July Bradley and I climbed the left wall, below the junction of the streams. The path we selected was up a gulch. After climbing for an hour we found ourselves in a vast amphitheater, and our way cut off. We clambered around to the left for half an hour until we found that we could not go up in that direction. Then we tried the rocks around to the right, and discovered a narrow shelf nearly half a mile long. In some places this was so wide that we passed along with ease; in others it was so narrow and sloping that we were compelled to lie down and crawl. We could look over the brink of the shelf down eight hundred feet and see the river rolling and plunging among the rocks. The edge of the cliff, five hundred feet above, seemed to blend with the sky. We went on until we came to a point where the wall was again broken down,

the verge overhead, and all the rocks, tinted with buff, gray, red, brown, and chocolate, never lichened, never moss-covered, but bare, and sometimes even polished. Strange, indeed, is "Toom-pin Woo-near Too-weap."

On the 17th of July we reached the junction of the Grand and Green, the head of the Colorado River.

Here we decided to go into camp for several days. The first day was spent in spreading our rations to dry, for we found them badly injured. The flour had been wet many times, and was now musty and full of hard lumps; so we made a sieve of mosquito bar and sifted it, losing more than two hundred pounds by the process. Our losses by the wrecking of the "No

and up this we climbed. On the right there was a narrow mural point of rocks extending toward the river, two or three hundred feet high, and six or eight hundred feet long. As last we came back to where this set in, and found it cut off from the main wall by a great crevice. Into this we passed, and now a long, narrow rock was between us and the river. The rock itself was split longitudinally and transversely, and the rains on the surface above had run down through the crevices and gathered into channels below, and then run off into the river. The crevices were usually narrow above, and, by erosion of the streams, wider below, forming a net-work of caves, but each cave having a narrow, winding sky-light up through the rocks. We wandered among these corridors for an hour or two, but found no place where the rocks were broken down so that we could climb up. At last we determined to attempt a passage by a crevice, and selected one which we thought wide enough to admit of the passage of our bodies, and yet narrow enough to climb out by pressing our hands and feet against the walls; so we climbed as men would out of a well. Bradley went first; I handed him the barometer, then climbed over his head, and he handed the barometer to me; so we passed each other alternately, until we emerged from the fissure on the summit of the rock.

What a world of grandeur was spread before us! Below was the cañon through which the Colorado runs; we could trace its course for miles, and at points catch glimpses of the river. From the north-west came the Green in a narrow, winding gorge. From the north-east came the Grand through a cañon that seemed, from where we stood, bottomless. Away to the west were lines of cliffs and ledges of rock; not such ledges as you may see where the quarryman splits his blocks, but ledges from which the gods might quarry mountains; not cliffs where you may see the swallow build its nest, but where the soaring eagle is lost to view before he reaches the summit. Between us and the distant cliffs were the strangely carved and pinnacled rocks of the "Toom-pin Woo-near Too-weap." Away to the east a group of eruptive mountains were seen—the Sierra La Sal. Their slopes were covered with pine, and deep gulches were flanked with great crags, and snow-fields were seen near the summits; so the mountains were in uniform— green, gray, and silver. Wherever we looked there was a wilderness of rocks—deep gorges where the rivers are lost below cliffs, and towers, and pinnacles, and ten thousand strangely carved forms in every direction, and beyond them mountains blending with the clouds.

We started again on the 21st of July, and found the river rough with bad rapids in close succession. In running one of these

the "Emma Dean" was swamped, and we were thrown into the river; but we clung to her, and in the first quiet water below she was righted and bailed out; but three of our oars were lost. The larger boats landed above the dangerous place and a portage was made. At night we camped on some rocks on the left bank under a cliff where we could scarcely find room to lie down.

And so progress was made from day to day with much labor, for we found many rapids and falls more difficult to master than any before. We named this "Cataract Cañon."

SIDE CAÑON IN GLEN CAÑON.

Midway down the cañon the more difficult cataracts were passed, the walls were found more regular, and the river, though swift, was rarely beset with rocks. The scenery was grand; there were many side cañons which we explored from time to time, always finding new wonders. I must describe one of these little excursions. One day Bradley, Captain Powell and myself went up one of the side cañons, entering it through a very narrow passage, having to wade along the course of a little stream until a cascade interrupted our progress. Then we climbed to the right for a hundred feet until we reached a little shelf along which we passed walking with great care, for it was narrow, until we passed around the fall. Here the gorge widened into a spacious sky-roofed chamber. In the farther end was a beautiful grove of cotton-woods, and between us and the cotton-woods the little stream widened out into three clear lakelets with bottoms of smooth rock. Beyond the cotton-woods the brook tumbled in a series of white, shining cascades, from heights that seemed immeasurable. Turning around, we could look through the cleft by which we came on the river and see towering walls beyond.

Our way the rest of that day was through a gorge, grand beyond description. We seemed to be in the depths of the earth and yet could look down into waters that reflected a bottomless abyss.

We arrived early in the afternoon at the head of more rapids and falls, but wearied with past work we determined to rest, and so we went into camp, and the afternoon and evening were spent by the men in discussing the probabilities of successfully navigating the river below. The barometric records were examined to see what descent we had made since we left the mouth of the Grand, and what descent since we left the Pacific Railroad, and what fall there yet must be to the river ere we reached the end of the great cañon. The conclusion at which they arrived was about this: that there were great descents yet to be made, but if they were distributed in rapids and short falls as they had been heretofore, we should be able to overcome them. But perhaps we should come to a fall in these cañons which we

The Heart of Cataract Cañon.

could not pass, where the walls would rise from the water's edge so that we could not land, and where the water would be so swift that we could not return. Places like this had been found, except that the falls were not so great as to prevent our running them with safety. But how would it be in the future?

By the 26th of July, we found our boats once more in a bad condition; they had been beaten so much against the rocks that they were leaking badly, so we lay over a day for repairs. About ten o'clock, Bradley, Powell, Howland, Hall and myself started up a side cañon to the east for the purpose of climbing out to a pine forest above where we hoped to obtain some pitch for our boats. We soon came to a pool of water, then to a brook, which was lost in the sands below; passing up the brook the cañon narrowed, the walls closed in and were often over-hanging. At last we found ourselves in a vast amphitheater with a pool of deep, clear, cold water on the bottom. At first our way seemed cut off, but we soon discovered a little shelf, along which we climbed, and, passing beyond the pool, walked a hundred yards or more, turned to the right and found ourselves in another amphitheater. There was a winding cleft at the top reaching out

to the country above, nearly two thousand feet overhead. The rounded, basin-shaped bottom was filled with water to the foot of the walls, and there was no shelf by which we could pass around to the foot; if we swam across, we met with a face of rock a hundred feet high, over which a little rill glided; and which it would be impossible to climb. We turned back and examined the walls on either side carefully, to discover, if possible, some other way of climbing out. In this search every man took his own course, and we were soon scattered. I almost abandoned the idea of getting out, and was engaged in searching for fossils, when I discovered, on the north, a broken place up which it might be possible for me to climb. The way for a distance was up a slide of rocks, then up an irregular wall by projecting points that formed steps and gave hand-hold, and then I reached a little shelf, along which I walked, and discovered a vertical fissure parallel to the face of the wall, and reaching to a higher shelf. This fissure was narrow, and I tried to climb up to the bench, which was about forty feet overhead, though I had a barometer on my back, which rather impeded my climbing. The walls of the fissure were of smooth lime-

REPAIRING BOATS
AT THE MOUTH
OF DIRTY DEVIL RIVER.

CLIMBING THE GRAND CAÑON.   by Thomas Moran

shuffling manner, a few inches at a time, until I had made perhaps twenty-five feet of the distance, when the crevice widened a little and I could not press my knees against the rocks in front with sufficient force to give me support in lifting my body. I tried to go back, but this I could not do without falling, so I struggled along, sidewise, farther into the crevice where it narrowed. By this time my muscles were exhausted and I could climb no longer, so I moved still a little farther into the crevice, where it was so narrow and wedging that I could lie in it, and there I rested. Five or ten minutes of this relief and up once more I pushed, till I reached the bench above. On this I could walk for a quarter of a mile, till I reached a place where the wall was again broken down so that I could climb up still farther. In an hour I reached the summit.

Hanging up my barometer to give it a few minutes to settle, I occupied myself in collecting resin from the piñon pines, which were found in great abundance. One of the principal objects of the climb was to get this resin for the purpose of smearing our boats, but I had with me no means of carrying it down. The day was very hot and my coat had been left in camp, so I had no linings to tear out, but it occurred to me to cut off the sleeve of my shirt and tie it up at one end, and in this little sack I collected about a gallon of pitch. After taking observations for altitude, I wandered back on the rocks for an hour or two, when, suddenly, I noticed that a storm was coming from the south. I sought a shelter in the rocks, but when the storm burst, it came down as a flood from the heavens,—not with gentle drops at first, slowly increasing in quantity, but as if suddenly poured from an immense basin. I was thoroughly drenched and almost washed away. It lasted not more than half-an-hour, when the clouds swept by to the north, and I was in the sunshine again.

In the meantime, I discovered a better way of getting down and started for camp, making the greatest haste possible. On reaching the bottom of the side cañon I found a thousand streams rolling down the cliffs on every side, carrying with them red sand, and these all united in the cañon below in one great stream of red mud. Traveling as fast as I could run, I soon reached the foot of the stream, for the rain did not reach the lower end of the cañon, and the water was running down a dry bed of sand; and although it came in waves several feet high and fifteen or twenty feet

stone, offering neither foot- nor hand-hold; so I supported myself by pressing my back against one wall and my knees against the other, and in this way lifted my body, in a in width, the sand soaked it up and it was lost. Wave followed wave and rolled along and was swallowed up, and still the floods came from above. I found I could travel faster than the stream, so I hastened on to camp and told the men there was a river coming down the cañon. We carried our camp equipage from the bank to where we the river was very swift, the cañon very tortuous, so that we could see but a few hundred yards ahead. The walls towered overhead, often overhanging so as to almost shut out the light. I stood on deck watching with intense anxiety, lest the way should lead us into danger, but we glided along with no obstruction, no falls, no rapids, and

by Thomas Moran

HEAD OF THE GRAND CAÑON—THE JUNCTION OF THE LITTLE AND THE GREAT COLORADO.

thought it would be above the water, and then stood by to see the river roll on to join the Colorado.

Near the foot of Cataract Cañon the walls suddenly closed in, so that the gorge was narrower than we had before seen it. The water filled it from wall to wall, giving no landing-place at the foot of the cliffs; in a mile and a half emerged from the narrow gorge into a more open and broken portion of the cañon. Now that it is past, it seems a very simple thing indeed to run through such a place; but the fear of what might be, made a deep impression upon all of us. Shortly after, we arrived at the foot of Cataract Cañon. Here a long cañon valley comes down from the east, and the river turns sharply to the west in a continuation of the line of the lateral valley. In the bend on the right vast numbers of crags, and pinnacles, and tower-shaped rocks are seen. We called it " Mille Crag Bend."

On the 29th of July, we entered a cañon with low red walls. A short distance below its head we discovered the ruins of an old building on the left wall. There is a narrow plain between the river and the wall just here, and on the brink of a rock two hundred feet high this old house stood. Its walls were of stone laid in mortar with much regularity. It was probably built three stories high; the lower story was yet almost intact, the second much broken down, and scarcely anything was left of the third. Great quantities of flint chips were found on the rocks near by, and many arrowheads, some perfect, others broken, and fragments of pottery were strewn about in great profusion. On the face of the cliff under the building, and along down the river for two or three hundred yards, there were many etchings. Two hours were given to the examination of these interesting ruins, wh 'n we ran down fifteen miles farther and disc overed another group.

The principal building was situated on the summit of the hill. Parts of the walls were standing to the height of eight or ten feet, and the mortar still remained in some places. The house was in the shape of an L, with five rooms on the ground floor; one in the angle and two in each extension. In the space in the angle there was a deep excavation. From what we knew of the people in the province of Tusayan, who are doubtless of the same race as the former inhabitants of these ruins, we concluded that this was a " Kiva" or underground chamber in which their religious ceremonies were performed.

The sandstone through which this cañon is cut is red and homogeneous, being the same as that through which Labyrinth Cañon runs. The smooth naked rock stretches out on either side of the river for many miles, but curiously carved mounds and cones are scattered everywhere, and deep holes are worn out. Many of these pockets were filled with water, and in one of these holes or wells, twenty feet deep, I found a tree growing. The excavation was so narrow I could step from its brink to a limb of the tree, and descend to the bottom of the well down a growing ladder. Many of these pockets are pot holes, being found in the course of little rills or brooks that run only during the rains which occasionally fall in this region, and often a few harder rocks, which evidently assisted in their excavation, could be found in their bottoms. Others which are shallower are not so easily explained. Perhaps they are found where softer spots existed in the sandstone, places that yielded more readily to atmospheric degradation, and where the loose sands were carried away by the winds.

Just before sundown I attempted to climb a rounded eminence, from which I hoped to obtain a good outlook over the surrounding country. It was formed of smooth mounds piled one above another, and up these I climbed, winding here and there to find a practicable way, until near the summit, when they became too steep for me to proceed. I searched about for a few minutes for a more easy way; what was my surprise at finding a stairway, evidently cut in the rock by human hands! At one place, where there is a vertical wall ten or twelve feet high, I found an old rickety ladder. It may be that this was a watch-tower of that ancient people whose homes we had found in ruins. On many of the tributaries of the Colorado I had before examined their deserted dwellings. Those that showed evidences of being built during the latter part of their occupation of the country were usually placed on the most inaccessible cliffs. Sometimes the mouths of caves had been walled across, and there were many other evidences showing their anxiety to secure defensible positions.

Probably the nomadic tribes were sweeping down upon them and they resorted to these cliffs and cañons for safety. It is not unreasonable to suppose that this orange mound was used as a watch-tower.

I stood where a lost people had lived centuries ago, and looked over the same strange country. I gazed off to great mountains in the north-west, slowly covered by the night until they were lost, and then turned toward camp. It was no easy task to find my way down the wall in the darkness, and I clambered about until nearly midnight, before I arrived there.

We made good progress the next day, as the water, though smooth, was swift. Sometimes the cañon walls were vertical to the top, sometimes vertical below with a mound-covered slope above, and in other places the slope with its mounds came down to the water's edge. Farther down we found the orange sandstone cut in two by a group of firm, calcareous strata, the lower bed underlaid by soft gypsiferous shales. Sometimes the upper, homogeneous bed was a smooth vertical wall, but usually it was carried into mounds with gently meandering valley lines. The lower bed, yielding to gravity as the softer shales below worked out into the river, broke into angular surfaces often having a columnar appearance. One could almost imagine that the walls had been carved with the purpose of representing giant architectural forms. In the deep recesses of the walls we found springs with mosses and ferns on the moistened sandstone.

RUNNING A RAPID.

Near our camp, below, there was a low, willow-covered strip of land along the wall on the east, and across this we walked to explore an alcove which was seen from the river. On entering we found a little grove of box-elder and cotton-wood trees, and, turning to the right, found ourselves in a vast chamber, carved out of the rocks. At the upper end there was a clear, deep pool of water bordered with verdure. Standing by the side of this and looking back, we could see the grove at the entrance. The chamber was more than two hundred feet high, five hundred feet long and two hundred feet wide. Through the ceiling and on through the rocks for a thousand feet above there was a narrow winding sky-light, and this was all carved out by a little stream which run during the few showers that fall now and then in that arid country. The waters, gathering rapidly on the bare rocks back of the cañon into a small channel, have carved a deep side cañon, through which they run until they fall into the farther end of this chamber. The rock at the ceiling is hard, the rock below very soft and friable, and having cut through the upper harder portion down into the lower and softer, these friable sandstones crumble and are washed out by the stream, and thus the chamber has been excavated.

Here we brought our camp, and when "Old Shady" sang us a song at night we were pleased to find this hollow in the rock filled with sweet sounds. It was doubtless made for an Academy of Music by a storm-born architect, so we named it "Music Temple."

Desirous of obtaining a view of the adjacent country, if possible, the men early the next morning rowed me across the river, and I passed along by the foot of the cliff half a mile up stream, and then climbed first up broken ledges, then two or three hundred yards up a smooth, sloping rock, and then passed out on a narrow ridge. Still I found that I had not attained an altitude from which I could overlook the region

by Thomas Moran

STANDING ROCKS ON POWELL'S PLATEAU.

outside of the cañon; so I descended into a little gulch, and climbed again to a higher ridge all the way along naked sandstone, and at last I reached a point of commanding view, where I could look several miles up the San Juan, and a long distance up the Colorado, and could see, away to the north-west, the Henry Mountains; to the north-east, the Sierra La Sal; to the southeast, unknown mountains, and to the southwest, the meanderings of the cañon. Then I returned to camp.

The features of this cañon are greatly diversified. Vertical walls are usually found to stand above great curves, and the river, sweeping around these bends, has undermined the cliffs in places; sometimes the rocks are overhanging. In other curves curious narrow glens are found. Into these we climbed by a rough stairway, perhaps several hundred feet, to where a spring burst out from under an overhanging cliff, and about the spring cotton-woods and willows stood, while along the curves of the brooklet oaks grew and other rich vegetation was seen, in marked contrast to the general

appearance of naked rock. Other wonderful features are the many side cañons or gorges that we passed; sometimes we stopped to explore these for a short distance.

In some places these walls are much nearer each other above than below, so that they looked somewhat like caves or chambers in the rocks. Usually in going up such a gorge we found beautiful vegetation, and our way was often cut off by deep basins or pot holes. On the walls back, and many miles into the country, numbers of monument-shaped buttes were observed, carved walls, royal arches, glens, alcove gulches, mounds, and monuments. From which of these features should we select a name? We finally named this "Glen Cañon."

Past these towering monuments, past these billows of orange sandstone, past these oak-set glens, fern-decked alcoves and mural curves, we glided hour after hour, stopping now and then as our attention was arrested by some new wonder, until we reached a point which is historical. In the year 1776, Father Escalante, a Spanish priest, made an expedition from Santa Fé to the north-west, crossing the Grand and Green, and then passing down the Wasatch Mountains and the southern plateaus, until he reached the Rio Virgen. His intention was to cross to the Mission of Monterey, but from information received from the Indians he decided that the route was impracticable. Not wishing to return to Santa Fé over the circuitous route by which he had just traveled, he attempted to go by one more direct, and which led him across the Colorado at a point known as El Vado de los Padres. From the description which we have read we were enabled to determine the place. A little stream comes down through a very narrow side cañon from the west. It was down this that he came, and our boats were brought up at the point where the ford crosses. A well-beaten Indian trail was seen here still. Between the cliff and the river there is a little meadow. The ashes of many camp fires were seen, and the bones of numbers of cattle were bleaching on the grass. For several years the Navajo Indians have raided on the Mormons who dwell in the valleys to the west, and doubtless cross frequently at this ford with their stolen cattle.

On the 5th of August, not without some feeling of anxiety, we entered a new cañon. By this time we had learned to closely observe the texture of the rock. In softer strata we had a quiet river; in harder, we found rapids and falls. Below us were the limestones and hard sandstones which we met in Cataract Cañon. This boded toil and danger. Besides the texture of the rocks there was another condition which affected the character of the channel, as we found by experience.

Where the strata were horizontal, the river was often quiet, and even though it might be very swift in places, no great obstacles were found. Where the rocks inclined in the direction traveled, the river usually swept with great velocity. But where the rocks dipped up stream, and the river cut obliquely across the upturned formations, harder strata above and softer below, then we must look out for rapids and falls.

Into hard rocks, and into rocks dipping up stream we passed, and started on a long, rocky, mad rapid. On the left there was vertical rock, and down by this cliff and around to the left we glided, just tossed enough by the waves to make us appreciate the rate at which we were traveling. The cañon was narrow, with vertical walls, which gradually grew higher, and more rapids and falls were found. We came to one with a drop of sixteen feet, around which we made a portage. A run of two miles, and then came another portage, long and difficult.

One day we came to a place where the river occupied the entire channel, and the walls were vertical from the water's edge. We saw a fall below and rowed up against the cliff. There was a little shelf, or rather a horizontal crevice, a few feet over our heads. One man stood on the deck of the boat, another climbed on his shoulders and then into the crevice. We passed him a line, and two or three others, with myself, followed and passed along the crevice until it became a shelf, as the upper part or roof was broken off. On this we walked for a short distance, slowly climbing all the way until we reached a point where the shelf was broken off, and we could go no farther. Then we went back to the boats, crossed the stream, got some logs that had lodged in the rocks, brought them to our side, passed them along the crevice and shelf, and bridged over this broken place. We went on to a point over the falls, but did not obtain a satisfactory view. Then we climbed out to the top of the wall and walked along to a point below the fall, from which it could be seen. It seemed possible

MONUMENT IN GLEN CAÑON.

to let our boats down with lines, to the head of the rapid, and then make a portage; so we returned, rowed down by the side of the cliff as far as we dared, and fastened one of the boats to a rock. Next we let another boat out to the end of its line beyond the first, and the third boat to the end of its line below the second, which brought it to the head of the fall, and under an overhanging rock. Then the upper boat, in obedience to a signal, let go; we pulled in the line and caught the nearest boat as it came, and then the last. Then we made our portage, and passed the fall.

On August 7th there was to be an eclipse of the sun, and Captain Powell and I started out early to climb the wall, taking our instruments with us, to determine our longi-

GLEN CAÑON.

by Thomas Moran

tude. Arriving at the summit after four hours' hard climbing to attain an altitude of two thousand feet, we built a platform of rocks on which to place our instruments, and waited for the eclipse, but clouds and rain came on, and sun and moon were obscured.

Much disappointed, we started on our return to camp, but it was late, and the clouds made the night very dark. We felt our way down among the rocks with great care for two or three hours, though making slow progress. At last we lost our way, and dared proceed no farther. The rain came down in torrents, and we could find no shelter. We could neither climb up nor go down, and in the darkness dared not move about but sat on the rocks and "weathered out" the long right.

The limestone of this cañon is often polished, and makes a beautiful marble. Sometimes the rocks are of many colors—white, gray, pink, and purple, with saffron tints. It was with very great labor that we made progress, meeting with many obstructions, running rapids, letting down our boats with lines from rock to rock, and sometimes carrying boats and cargoes around bad places. At one place we camped, after a hard portage, under an overhanging wall, glad to find shelter from the rain, and equally glad to find a few sticks of drift-wood just sufficient to boil a pot of coffee. The water sweeps rapidly in this elbow of river and has cut its way under the rock, excavating a vast half-circular chamber, which, if utilized for a theater, would give sitting for fifty thousand people. Objections might be urged against it from the fact that at high water the floor is covered with a raging flood.

Soon after passing this point the scenery was on a grand scale. The walls of the cañon, twenty-five hundred feet high, were of marble of many beautiful colors, often polished below by the waves, or far up the sides where showers had washed the sands over the cliffs. At one place I had a walk, for more than a mile, on a marble pavement all polished and fretted with strange devices, and embossed in a thousand fantastic patterns. Through a cleft in the wall the sun shone on this pavement, which gleamed in iridescent beauty. Up into this cleft I found my way. It was very narrow, with a succession of pools standing at higher levels as I went back. The water in these pools was clear and cool, coming down from springs. Then I returned to the pavement, which was but a terrace or bench over which

the river ran at its flood, but left bare at this time. Along the pavement in many places were basins of clear water, in strange contrast to the red mud of the river. At length I came to the end of this marble terrace, and jumped aboard the boat. Riding down a short distance a beautiful view was presented. The river turned sharply to the east, and seemed inclosed by a wall set with a million brilliant gems. What could it mean!—every one wondered. On coming nearer we found a fountain bursting from the rock high overhead, and the spray in the sunshine formed the gems which bedecked the walls. The rocks below the fountain were covered with mosses and ferns and many beautiful flowering plants. We named it "Vasey's Paradise," in honor of the botanist who traveled with us the previous year.

When it rains in these cañons scarcely do the first drops fall ere little rills are formed and run down the walls; as the storms come on the rills increase in size, until they become streams. Although the walls of this cañon are chiefly limestone, the country adjacent is of red sandstone, and the waters loaded with these sands come in rivers of bright red mud, leaping over the walls in innumerable cascades. It is easy to see why these walls present a polished surface in many places.

We had cut through the sandstones and limestones met in the upper part of this cañon, and through one great bed of marble a thousand feet in thickness. In this, great numbers of caves are hollowed out, and carvings are seen which suggest architectural forms, though on a scale so grand that architectural terms belittle them.

As this great bed forms a distinctive feature of the cañon, we called it Marble Cañon. Along the walls many projections are set out into the river as if they were buttressed for support. The walls themselves are half a mile high, and these buttresses are on a corresponding scale, jutting into the river scores of feet. In the recesses between these projections there are quiet bays of water, except at the foot of a rapid, when they become dancing eddies and whirlpools. Sometimes these alcoves have caves at the back, giving them the appearance of great depth; then other caves were seen above, forming vast dome-shaped chambers; walls and buttresses and chambers are all of marble.

On August 10th, we reached the mouth of the Colorado Chiquito, the foot of Mar-

by Thomas Moran

MARBLE CAÑON.

ble Cañon. This stream enters through a cañon on a scale quite as grand as that of the Colorado itself. It is a very small river, and exceedingly muddy and salt. I walked up the stream three or four miles, crossing and recrossing where I could easily wade it; then I climbed several hundred feet at one place and could see up the chasm, through which the river ran for several miles.

I walked down the gorge to the left, at the foot of the cliff climbed to a bench overhead, and discovered a trail deeply worn in the rock; where it crossed the side gulches, in some places steps had been cut. I could see no evidence of its having been traveled for a long time, and it was doubtless a path used by the people who inhabited this region anterior to the present Indian races, —the people who built the communal houses of which mention has been made.

Upon my return to camp the men told me they had discovered ruins and many fragments of pottery. also etchings and hieroglyphics on the rocks. We found, on comparing the readings of the barometers above and below, that the walls were about three thousand feet high—or more than half a mile.

On August 13th we were ready once more to start on our way down the Great Unknown. Our boats, tied to a stake, were chafing each other as they were tossed by the fretful river. They rode high and buoyant, for their loads were lighter than we could desire, indeed we had but a month's rations remaining. The flour had been resifted through the mosquito-net sieve; the spoiled bacon had been dried, and the worst of it boiled; the few pounds of dried apples had been spread in the sun, and had shrunk to their normal bulk; the sugar had all melted and gone on its way down the river, but we had a large sack of coffee.

The lightening of the boats had this advantage, we thought—they would ride the waves better, and we would have but little to carry when we made a portage.

We were three-quarters of a mile down in the depths of the earth, and the great river shrunk into insignificance as it dashed its angry waves against the walls and cliffs that rose to the world above; they were but puny ripples, and we but pygmies running up and down the sands, or lost among the bowlders. We had an unknown distance yet to run, an unknown river yet to explore; what falls there were we knew not, what rocks beset the channel we knew not. The men

talked as cheerfully as ever, jests were bandied about freely, but to me the cheer was somber, the jests were ghastly.

With some eagerness and some anxiety, we entered the cañon below and were carried along by swift water, through walls which rose from its very edge. They had the same structure as we noticed the day before, tiers of irregular shelves below, and above these, steep slopes to the foot of marble cliffs.

We ran six miles in little more than half-an-hour, and emerged into a more open portion of the cañon, where high hills and ledges of rock intervened between the river and the distant walls. Just at the head of the open place the river ran across a dike,

by Thomas Moran
THE SPANISH BAYONET IN MARBLE CAÑON.

that is, a fissure in the rocks open to depths below, which has been filled with eruptive matter, which on cooling became harder than the rocks through which the fissure was made. When these were washed away the harder volcanic matter remained as a wall. The river cuts a gate-way through this, several hundred feet high and as many wide. As it crosses the wall there is a fall below and a bad rapid filled with bowlders of trap, so we were compelled to stop and make a portage.

At daybreak one morning we walked down the bank of the river on a little sandy beach, to take a view of a new feature in the cañon. Heretofore hard rocks had given us a bad river; soft rocks, smooth water. A series of rocks harder than any we experienced now began. The river entered the granite!* We could see but a little way into

* Geologists would call these rocks metamorphic crystalline schists, with dikes and beds of granite; but we will use the popular name for the whole series—granite.

the granite gorge, but it looked threatening. After breakfast we continued our perilous voyage. The cañon was narrower than we had ever before seen it; the water was swift; there were but few broken rocks in the channel, but the walls were set on either side with pinnacles, and crags and sharp angular buttresses, bristling with wind- and wave-polished spires, extended far out into the river. Ledges of rock jutted into the stream, their tops sometimes just below the surface, sometimes rising few or many feet above, and island ledges, and island pinnacles, and island towers broke the swift course of the stream into chutes, and eddies, and whirlpools. We soon reached a place where a creek came in from the left, and just below the channel was choked with bowlders which had washed down the lateral cañon and formed a dam, over which there was a fall of thirty or forty feet; but on the bowlders we could get foothold, and here we made a portage. Three more such

GRANITE WALLS.

dams were found; over one we made a portage; at the other two we found chutes through which we could run.

About eleven o'clock of the same day we heard a great roar ahead, and approached it very cautiously, the sound growing louder and louder as we ran. At last we found ourselves above a long, broken fall, with ledges and pinnacles of rock obstructing the river. There was a descent of seventy-five or eighty feet, perhaps, in a third of a mile, and the rushing waters were broken into great waves on the rocks, and lashed themselves into foam. We could land just above, but there was no foothold on either side by which a portage could be made. It was nearly a thousand feet to the top of the granite, so it was impossible to carry our boats around, though we could climb to that point ourselves by a side gulch, and passing along a mile or two, could descend to the river. We discovered this on examination, but such a portage would have been impracticable for us, and we were obliged to run the rapid or abandon the river.

We did not hesitate, but stepped into the boats, pushed off, and dashed away, first on smooth but swift water, then striking a glassy wave and riding to its top, down again into the trough, up again on a higher wave, and down and up on the waves, higher and still higher, until we struck one just as it curled back, when a breaker rolled over our little undaunted boat. On we sped, till the boat was caught in a whirlpool and spun around and around. When we managed to pull out again, the other boats had passed us. The open compartment of the " Emma Dean" was filled with water, and every breaker rolled over us. Hurled back from the rock now on this side, now on that, we were carried at last into an eddy, in which we struggled for a few minutes, and then out again, the breakers still rolling over us. Our boat was unmanageable, but she could not sink, and we drifted down another hundred yards through breakers—how, we scarcely knew. We found the other boats had turned into an eddy at the foot of the fall, and were waiting to catch us as we came, for they had seen that our boat was swamped. They pushed out as we came near, and pulled us in against the wall. We bailed out the boat and started on again.

Figure 59.—Horse-Shoe Cañon.

THE GRAND CAÑON OF THE COLORADO.

(THIRD PAPER.)

THE walls were now more than a mile in height. Stand on the south steps of the Treasury Building in Washington and look down Pennsylvania Avenue to the Capitol Park, measure the distance with your eye, and imagine cliffs extending to that altitude, and you will understand what I mean. Or, stand at Canal Street in New York and look up Broadway to Grace Church, and you have about the distance; stand at Lake Street Bridge in Chicago and look down to the Union Dépôt, and you have it again.

A thousand feet of this is up through granite crags, then slopes and perpendicular cliffs rise one above the other to the summit. The gorge is black and narrow below, red and gray and flaring above, and crags and angular projections on walls which, cut in many places by side cañons, seem to be a vast wilderness of rocks. Down through these gloomy depths we glided, always listening; for the mad waters kept up their roar; always watching and peering ahead—for the narrow cañon was winding and the river was closed so that we could see but a few hundred yards, and what might be below we knew not. We strained our ears for warning

of the falls and watched for rocks, or stopped now and then in the bay of a recess to admire the gigantic scenery; and ever as we went, there was some new pinnacle or tower, some crag or peak, some distant view of the upper plateau, some deep, narrow side cañon, or some strangely shaped rock. On we went, through this solemn, mysterious way. The river was very deep, the cañon very narrow and still obstructed, so that there was no steady flow of the stream, but the waters wheeled, and rolled, and boiled, and we were scarcely able to determine where we could go with greatest safety. Now the boat was carried to the right, perhaps close to the wall, again she was shot into the stream and dragged over to the other side, where, caught in a whirlpool, she spun about like a chip. We could neither land nor run as we pleased; the boats were entirely unmanageable; now one, now another was ahead, each crew looking after its own safety.

We came to another rapid; two of the boats ran it perforce; one succeeded in landing, but there was no foothold by which to make a portage, and she was pushed out again into the stream; the next minute a

THE INNER GORGE.

great reflex wave filled the open compartment; she was water-logged, and drifted at the mercy of the waters. Breaker after breaker rolled over her, and one tossed her deck downward. The men were thrown out, but they clung to the boat, and she drifted down alongside of us, and we were able to catch her. She was soon bailed out and the men were aboard once more, but the oars were lost; their place being supplied by a pair from the " Emma Dean."

Clouds were playing in the cañon that day. Sometimes they rolled down in great masses, filling the gorge with gloom; sometimes they hung above from wall to wall, covering the cañon with a roof of impending storm, and we could peer long distances up and down this cañon corridor, with its cloud roof overhead, its walls of black granite, and its river bright with the sheen of broken waters. Then a gust of wind would sweep down a side gulch and make a rift in the clouds, revealing the blue heavens, and a stream of sunlight poured in. Again the clouds drifted away into the distance and hung around crags and peaks, and pinnacles, and towers, and walls, covering them with a mantle that lifted from time to time and set them all in sharp relief. Then baby clouds crept out of side cañons, glided around points, and crept back again into more distant gorges. Other clouds stretched in strata across the cañon, with intervening vista views to cliffs and rocks beyond.

Then the rain came down. Little rills were formed rapidly above; these soon grew into brooks, and the brooks into creeks, which tumbled over the walls in innumerable cascades, adding their wild music to the roar of the river. When the rain ceased, the rills, brooks, and creeks ran dry. The waters that fall during the rain on these steep rocks are gathered at once into the river; they could scarcely be poured in more suddenly if some vast spout ran from the clouds to the stream itself. When a storm bursts over the cañon a side gulch is a dangerous place, for a sudden flood may come, and the inpouring water raise the river so as to drown the rocks before your very eyes.

On the 16th of August we were compelled to stop once more and dry our rations and make oars.

The Colorado is never a clear stream, and, owing to the rains which had been falling for three or four days, and the floods which were poured over the walls, bringing down great quantities of mud, it was now exceedingly turbid. A little affluent entered opposite our camp—a clear, beautiful creek, or river, as it would be termed in the Western country, where streams are not so abundant. We had named one stream, above, in honor of the great chief of the bad angels, and as this was a beautiful contrast to that, we concluded to name it " Bright Angel River."

In a little gulch just above the creek, I discovered the ruins of two or three old houses, which were originally of stone laid in mortar. Only the foundations were left, but irregular blocks, of which the houses were constructed, were scattered about. In one room I found an old mealing stone, deeply worn, as if it had been much used. A great deal of pottery was strewn about, and old trails were seen, which, in some places, were deeply worn into the rock. It was ever a source of wonder to us why these ancient people sought such inaccessible places for their homes. They were doubtless an agricultural race, but there were no lands here of any considerable extent which they could have cultivated. To the west of Oraiby, one of the towns in the Province of Tusayan, in northern Arizona, the inhabitants have actually built little terraces along the face of the cliff, where a spring gushes out, and there made their site for gardens. It is possible that the ancient inhabitants of this place made their agricultural lands in the same way. But why should they seek such spots ? Surely the country was not so crowded with population as to demand the utilization of a region like this. The only solution which suggests itself is this: We know that for a century or two after the settlement of Mexico, many expeditions were sent into the country now comprised in Arizona and New Mexico, for the purpose of bringing the town-building people under the dominion of the Spanish Government. Many of their villages were destroyed, and the inhabitants fled to regions at that time unknown, and there are traditions among the people who now inhabit the pueblos which still remain, that the cañons were these unknown lands. It may be that these buildings were erected at that time. Sure it is that they had a much more modern appearance than the ruins scattered over Nevada, Utah, Colorado, Arizona and New Mexico. These old Spanish conquerors had a monstrous greed for gold, and a wonderful lust for saving souls. Treasure they must have, if not on earth, why, then in heaven; and when they failed to find heathen temples bedecked with silver they propitiated heaven

by Thomas Moran

GRANITE FALLS, KIABAB DIVISION, GRAND CANYCN

THE GRAND CAÑON, AT THE FOOT OF TO-RÓ-WEAP, LOOKING WEST.   by Thomas Moran

by seizing the heathens themselves. There is yet extant a copy of a record made by a heathen artist to express his conception of the demands of the conquerors. In one part of the picture we have a lake, and near by stands a priest pouring water on the head of a native. On the other side a poor Indian has a cord about his throat. Lines run from these two groups to a central figure, a man with a beard and full Spanish panoply. The interpretation of the picture writing is this: "Be baptized as this saved heathen, or be hanged as that damned heathen."

Doubtless some of these people preferred a third alternative, and rather than be baptized or hanged, they chose to be imprisoned within these cañon walls.

Our rations were rapidly spoiling, the bacon being so badly injured that we were compelled to throw it away, and our saleratus had been lost overboard. We had now plenty of coffee, but only musty flour sufficient for ten days, and a few dried apples. We must make all haste possible. If we met with difficulties as we had done in the cañon above, we should be compelled to give up the expedition and try to reach the Mormon settlements to the north. Our hopes were that the worst places were passed, but our barometers were so badly injured as to be useless, so we had lost our reckoning in altitude, and knew not how much descent the river had yet to make.

It rained from time to time, sometimes all day, and we were thoroughly drenched and chilled, but between showers the sun shone with great power, and the mercury stood at 115°, so that we had rapid changes from great extremes, which were very disagreeable. It was especially cold in the rain at night. The little canvas we had was rotten and useless; the rubber ponchos, with which we started from Green River City, were all lost; more than half the party were without hats, and not one of us had an entire suit of clothes, nor had we a blanket apiece. So we gathered drift-wood and built fires, but the rain came down in torrents and extinguished them, and we sat up all night on the rocks shivering. We were, indeed, much more exhausted by the night's discomfort than by the day's toil.

So difficult were the portages on August 18th that we advanced but two miles in this work. I climbed up the granite to its summit and went back over the rust-colored sandstones and greenish-yellow shales to the foot of the marble wall. I climbed so high that the men and boats were lost in the black depths below, and

the river was but a rippling brook, and still there was more cañon above than below.

I pushed on to an angle where I hoped to get a view of the country beyond, to see, if possible, what the prospect was of our soon running through this plateau, or, at least, of meeting with some geological change that would let us out of the granite; but, arriving at the point, I could see below only a labyrinth of deep gorges.

MU-AV CAÑON, LOOKING WEST.　by Thomas Moran

After dinner, in running a rapid, the pioneer boat was upset by a wave. We were some distance in advance of the larger boats; the river was rough and swift and we were unable to land; so we clung to the boat and were carried down stream over another rapid. The men in the boats above saw our trouble, but were caught in whirlpools, and went spinning about so in the eddies that it seemed a long time before they came to our relief. At last they came. The boat was turned right side up and bailed out, the oars, which, fortunately, had floated along in company with us, were gathered up, and on we went without even landing.

On the 20th, the characteristics of the cañon changed; the river was broader, the walls were sloping, and composed of black slates that stood on edge. These nearly

GRAND CAÑON, FROM TO-RÓ-WEAP, LOOKING EAST.   by Thomas Moran

much smaller scale than the great bays and buttresses of Marble Cañon. The river was still rapid, and we stopped to let down with lines several times, but made greater progress, running ten miles.

On a terrace of trap we discovered another group of ruins. Evidently, there was once quite a village here. Again we found mealing-stones and much broken pottery, and upon a little natural shelf in the rock, back of the ruins, we found a globular basket that would hold perhaps a third of a bushel. It was badly broken, and, as I attempted to take it up, it fell to pieces. There were many beautiful flint chips scattered about, as if this had been the home of an old arrow-maker.

The next day, in nearing a curve, we heard a mad roar, and down we were carried with a dizzying velocity to the head of another rapid. On either side, high over our heads, there were overhanging granite walls, and the sharp bends cut off our view. A few moments and we should be carried into unknown waters. Away we went on a long, winding chute. I stood on deck, supporting myself with a strap fastened on either side to the gunwale, and the boat glided rapidly where the water was smooth. Striking a wave, she leaped and bounded like a thing of life, and we had a wild ride for ten miles, which we made in less than one hour. The excitement was so great that we forgot the danger until we heard the roar of a great fall below, when we backed on our oars, and were carried slowly toward its head, and succeeded in landing just above. We found we could make a portage, and at this we were engaged for some hours.

Just here we ran out of the granite. Good cheer returned; we forgot the storms and the gloom, and the cloud-covered cañons, and the raging of the river, and pushed our boats from shore in great glee.

The next day we came to rapids again, over which we were compelled to make a

vertical slates are washed out in places; that is, the softer beds are washed out between the harder, which are left standing. In this way curious little alcoves are formed, in which are quiet bays of water, but on a portage. While the men were thus employed I climbed the wall on the north-east to a height of about 2,500 feet, where I could obtain a good view of a long stretch of cañon below. Its course was to the south-west. The walls seemed to rise very abruptly for 2,500 or 3,000 feet, and then there was a gentle sloping terrace on each side for two or three miles, and then cliffs rising from 1,500 to 2,500 feet. From the brink of these the plateau stretches back to the north and south for a long distance. Away down the cañon on the right wall I could see a group of mountains, some of which appeared to stand on the brink of the cañon. The effect of the terrace was to give the appearance of a narrow, winding valley with high walls on either side, and a deep, dark, meandering gorge down its middle. It was impossible from this point of view to determine whether there was granite at the bottom or not; but from geological considerations I concluded we should have marble walls below, and this proved to be the case, except that here and there we passed through patches of granite, like hills thrust up into the limestone. At one of

one beautiful fall of more than a hundred and fifty feet, and climbed around it to the right on broken rocks. As I proceeded the cañon narrowed very much, being but fifteen or twenty feet wide, the walls rising on

MARBLE PINNACLE IN KANAB CAÑON.   by Thomas Moran

these places we made another portage, and, taking advantage of this delay, I went up a little stream to the north, wading all the way, sometimes having to plunge in to my neck, and in other places to swim across little basins that had been excavated at the foot of the walls. Along its course were many cascades and springs gushing out from the rocks on either side. Sometimes a cottonwood tree grew over the water. I came to

either side many hundreds of feet—perhaps thousands.

In some places the stream had not excavated its channel vertically through the rocks, but had cut obliquely, so that one wall overhung the other. In other places it was cut vertically above and obliquely below, or obliquely above and vertically below, so that it was impossible to see out overhead. But I could go no farther. The

KANAB CANYON, NEAR THE JUNCTION.

KANAB CANYON, IN THE RED WALL LIMESTONE.

time which I estimated it would take to make the portage had now almost expired, so I started back on a round trot, wading in the creek and plunging through basins, and finding the men waiting for me.

Farther on we passed a stream which leaped into the Colorado by a direct fall of more than a hundred feet, forming a beautiful cascade. There was a bed of very hard rock above, thirty or forty feet in thickness, and there were much softer beds below. The harder beds above project many yards beyond the softer, which are washed out, forming a deep cave behind the fall, and the stream poured through a narrow crevice above into a deep pool below. Around on the rocks, in the cave-like chamber, were set beautiful ferns with delicate fronds and enameled stalks; the little frondlets had their points turned down to form spore-cases. It had much the appearance of the maidenhair fern, but was larger. This delicate foliage covered the rocks all about the fountain and gave the chamber great beauty.

It was curious to see how anxious we were to make up our reckoning every time we stopped, now that our diet was confined to plenty of coffee, a very little spoiled flour, and a very few dried apples. It had come to be a race for a dinner. On the 23d, we ran twenty-two miles, and on the 24th, twenty miles. Such fine progress put all hands in good cheer, but not a moment of daylight was lost, and on the 25th, though we were retarded by a portage, we made thirty-five miles.

During this last day we passed monuments of lava standing in the river, mostly low rocks, but some of them shafts more than a hundred feet high. Three or four miles farther down these increased in number. Great quantities of cooled lava and many cinder-cones were seen on either side, and then we came to an abrupt cataract. Just over the fall on the right wall a cinder-cone, or extinct volcano with a well-defined crater, stands on the very brink of the cañon. From the volcano vast floods of lava have been poured down into the river, and a stream of the molten rock has run up three or four miles, and down we knew not how far. Just where it poured over the cañon wall is the fall. The whole north side as far as we could see was lined with black basalt, and high up on the opposite wall were patches of the same material resting on the benches and filling old alcoves and caves, giving to the wall a spotted appearance. The rocks are broken in two along a line

which here crosses the river, and the beds which we had traced coming down the cañon for thirty miles have dropped 800 feet on the lower side of the line, forming what geologists call a fault.

The volcanic cone stands directly over the fissure thus formed. On the side of the river opposite, mammoth springs burst out of this crevice one or two hundred feet above the river, pouring in a stream quite equal to the Colorado Chiquito. This stream seemed to be loaded with carbonate of lime, and the water flowing away leaves an incrustation on the rocks, and this process has been continued for a long time, for extensive deposits are noticed in which are basins with bubbling springs. The water is salt.

As we floated along I was able to observe the wonderful phenomena relating to this flood of lava. The cañon was doubtless filled to a height of twelve or fifteen hundred feet, perhaps by more than one flood. This would dam the water back, and in cutting through this great lava-bed a new channel has been formed, sometimes on one side, sometimes on the other. The cooled lava, being of firmer texture than the rocks of which the walls are composed, in some places remains; in others a narrow channel has been cut, leaving a line of basalt on either side. It is possible that the lava cooled faster on the sides against the walls, and that the center ran out; but this is only conjecture. There are other places where almost the whole of the lava is gone, only patches of it being seen where it has caught on the walls. As we proceeded we could see that it ran out into side cañons. In some places this basalt has a fine columnar structure, often in concentric prisms, and masses of these columns have coalesced. In places, when the flow occurred, the cañon was probably at about the same depth as it is now, for we could see where the basalt rolled out on the sand, and what seemed curious to me, the sands were not metamorphosed to any appreciable extent. At places the bed of the river is of sandstone or limestone, in others of lava, showing that it has all been cut out again where the sandstone and limestone appear, but there is a little yet left where the bed is of lava.

What a conflict of water and fire there must have been here! Imagine a river of molten rock running down into a river of melted snow!

Up to this time, since leaving the Colorado Chiquito, we had seen no evidence that the Indians inhabiting the plateaus on either side ever approached the river, but one morning we discovered an Indian garden at using the water which burst out in springs at the foot of the cliffs for irrigation. The corn was looking quite well, though not sufficiently advanced to give us roasting ears; but there were some nice green squashes. We carried ten or a dozen of these on board our boats, and hurriedly left, not willing to be caught in the robbery. We excused ourselves on the plea of our great want. We ran down a short distance to where we felt certain no Indians could follow, and what a kettle of squash sauce we made! True, we had no salt with which to season it, but it made a fine addition to our unleavened bread and coffee. Never was fruit so sweet to us as those stolen squashes.

At night we found, on making up our reckoning, that we had again run thirty-five miles during the day. What a supper we made — unleavened bread, green squash sauce, and strong coffee! We had been for a day or two on half rations, but now we had no stint of roast squash. A few more days like this and we should be out of prison.

On the 27th the river took a more southerly direction. The dip of the rocks was to the north, and we were rapidly running into the lower formation. Unless our course changed we

SIDE GULCH IN GRAND CAÑON.　　by Thomas Moran

the foot of the wall on the right, just where a little stream, with a narrow flood-plain, came down through a side cañon. Along the valley the Indians had planted corn, should very soon run again into the granite,—which gave us some anxiety. Now and then the river turned to the west, and gave birth to hopes that were soon destroyed by another turn to the south. About nine o'clock we came to the dreaded rock. It was with no little misgiving that we saw the river enter those black, hard walls. At the very entrance we were compelled to make a portage, after which we had to let down with lines past some ugly rocks.

At eleven o'clock we came to a place in the river which seemed much worse than any we had met in all its course. A little creek came down from the right, and another, just opposite, from the left. We landed first on the right, and clambered up over the granite pinnacles for a mile or two, but could see no way by which we could let down, and to run it would be sure destruction. Then we crossed to examine it on the left. High above the river we could walk along on the top of the granite, which was broken off at the edge and set with crags and pinnacles, so that it was very difficult to get a view of the river at all. In my eagerness to reach a point where I could see the roaring fall below, I went too far on the wall, and could neither advance nor retreat, and stood with one foot on a little projecting rock and clung, with my hand fixed in a little crevice. Finding I was caught here, suspended four hundred feet above the river, into which I should fall if my footing failed, I called for help. The men came and passed me a line, but I could not let go the rock long enough to take hold of it; then they brought two or three of the longest oars. All this took time, which seemed very precious to me. But at last the blade of one of the oars was pushed into a little crevice in the rock beyond me in such a manner that they could hold me pressed against the wall. Then another was fixed in such a

way that I could step on it, and I was rescued.

The whole afternoon was spent in examining the river below by clambering among the crags and pinnacles. We found that the lateral stream had washed bowlders into the river so as to form a dam, over which the river made a broken fall of eighteen or twenty feet; then there was a rapid, beset with rocks for two or three hundred yards, while on the sides points of the wall projected into the river. There was a second fall below, how great we could not tell, and below that a rapid filled with huge rocks for two or three hundred yards. At the bottom of this, from

OUR MESSENGER.

the right wall, a great rock projected half-way across the river. It had a sloping surface extending up stream, and the water, coming down with all the momentum gained in the falls and rapids above, rolled up this inclined plane many feet and tumbled over to the left.

I decided that it would be possible to let down over the first fall, then run near the right cliff to a point just above the second, where we could pull out into a little chute, and, having run over that in safety, to pull with all our power across the stream to avoid the great rock below. On my return to the boats, I announced to the men that we were to run it the next morning.

After supper Captain Howland asked to have a talk with me. We walked up a little creek a short distance, and I soon found that his object was to remonstrate against my determination to proceed; he thought we had better abandon the river here. I learned that his brother, William Dunn and himself had determined to go no farther in the boats. We returned to camp, but nothing was said to the other men.

During the two days previous our course had not been plotted, so I sat down and did this for the purpose of finding where we were by dead reckoning. It was a clear night, and I took out the sextant to make observations for latitude, and found that the astronomic determination agreed very nearly with that of the plot—quite as closely as might be expected from a meridian observation on a planet. I concluded we must be about forty-five miles in a direct line from the mouth of the Rio Virgen. If we could reach that point, we knew there were settlements up that river about twenty miles. This forty-five miles in a direct line would probably be eighty or ninety in the meandering line of the river. But then we knew that there was a comparatively open country for many miles above the mouth of the Virgen, which was our point of destination.

As soon as I determined all this I spread my plot on the sand and awoke Howland, who was sleeping down by the river, and showed him where I supposed we were, and where several Mormon settlements were situated. We had another short talk about the morrow, and he lay down again.

But for me there was no sleep; all night long I paced up and down a little path on a few yards of sand beach along the river. Was it wise to go on? I went to the boats again to look at our rations. I felt

satisfied we could get over the danger immediately before us; what there might be below I knew not. From our outlook on the cliffs the cañon seemed to make another great bend to the south, and this, from our previous experience, meant more and higher

OUR MESSENGER'S BOY.

granite walls. I was not sure we could climb the walls of the cañon here, and I knew enough of the country to be certain, when at the top of the wall, that it was a desert of rocks and sand between this and the nearest Mormon settlement, which on the most direct line must have been seventy-five miles away. True, I believed that the late rains were favorable to us, should we go out; for the probabilities were that we should find water still standing in holes. At one time I almost made up my mind to leave the river. But for years I had been contemplating this trip. To leave the exploration unfinished,—to say there was a part of this cañon which we could not explore, having already almost accomplished the undertaking,—I could not reconcile myself to this.

AN ALCOVE IN THE RED WALL.

NICHES OR PANELS IN THE RED WALL LIMESTONE.

The panels are over six hundred feet high.

Then I awoke my brother and told him of Howland's determination. He, at least, promised to stay with me. Next I called up Hawkins, the cook, and he made a like promise; then Sumner, Bradley, and Hall, and they all agreed to go on.

At last daylight came and we had breakfast, without a word being said about the future. The meal was as solemn as a funeral. After breakfast I asked the three men if they still thought it best to leave us. The elder Howland thought it was, and Dunn agreed with him; the younger Howland tried to persuade them to go on with the party, failing in which, he decided to go with his brother.

Then we crossed the river. The small boat was very much disabled and unseaworthy. With the loss of hands consequent on the departure of the three men we should not be able to run all the boats, so I decided to leave the " Emma Dean." Two rifles and a shot-gun were given to the men who were going out. I asked them to help themselves to the rations and take what they thought to be a fair share. This they refused to do, saying they had no fear but that they could get something to eat; but Billy, the cook, had a pan of biscuits prepared for dinner, and these he left on a rock.

Before starting we took our barometers, fossils, minerals, and some ammunition, and left them on the rocks. We were going over this place as light as possible. The three men helped us lift our boats over a rock twenty-five or thirty feet high, and let them down again over the first falls. Just before leaving I wrote a letter to my wife and gave it to Howland. Sumner gave him his watch, directing that it be sent to his sister, should he not be heard from again.

The records of the expedition had been kept in duplicate, and one set of these was given to Howland; and now we were ready to start. For the last time they entreated us not to go on, and told us that to go on was madness; that we could never get through safely; that the river turned again to the south into the granite, and a few miles of such rapids and falls would exhaust our entire stock of rations, when it would be too late to climb out. It was rather a solemn parting and some tears were shed, for each party thought the other was taking the dangerous course.

My old boat having been deserted, I went on board " The Maid of the Cañon." The three men climbed a crag that overhung the river, to watch us off. The " Maid " pushed out, we glided rapidly along the foot of the wall, just grazing one great rock, pulled out a little into the chute of the second fall, and plunged over it. The open compartment was filled when we struck the first wave below, but we cut through it, and then the men pulled with all their power toward the left wall and swung clear of the dangerous rock below.

We were scarcely a minute in running it, and found that, although it looked bad from above, we had passed many places that were worse. The other boat followed without more difficulty.

We landed at the first practicable point below, fired our guns as a signal to the men above that we had gone over in safety, and remained a couple of hours, hoping they would take the smaller boat and follow us. We were behind a curve in the cañon and could not see up to where we left them. As they did not come we pushed on again. Until noon we had a succession of rapids and falls, all of which we ran in safety.

Just after dinner we came to another bad place. A little stream came in from the left, and below there was a fall, and still below another fall. Above, the river tumbled down over and among the rocks in whirlpools and great waves, and the waters were white with foam. We ran along the left, above this, and soon saw that we could not get down on that side, but it seemed possible to let down on the other, so we pulled up stream for two or three hundred yards and crossed. There was a bed of basalt on this northern side of the cañon, with a bold escarpment that seemed to be a hundred feet high. We could climb it and walk along its summit to a point where we were just at the head of the fall. Here the basalt seemed to be broken down again, and I directed the men to take a line to the top of the cliff and let the boats down along the wall. One man remained in the boat to keep her clear of the rocks and prevent her line from being caught on the projecting angles. I climbed the cliff and passed along to a point just over the fall, and descended by broken rocks, and found that the break of the fall was above the break of the wall, so that we could not land, and that still below the river was very bad, and there was no possibility of a portage. Without waiting farther to examine and determine what should be done, I hastened back to the top of the cliff to stop the boats from coming down. When I arrived I found the men had let one of them down to the head of

HEAD OF THE GRAND CANYON.

the fall; she was in swift water and they were not able to pull her back, nor were they able to go on with the line, as it was not long enough to reach the higher part of the cliff which was just before them; so they took a bight around a crag, and I sent two men back for the other line. The boat was in very swift water, and Bradley was standing in the open compartment holding out his oar to prevent her from striking against the foot of the cliffs. Now she shot out into the stream and up as far as the line would permit, and then wheeling, drove headlong against the rock; then out and back again, now straining on the line, now striking against the cliff. As soon as the second line was brought we passed it down to him, but his attention was all taken up with his own situation, and he did not see what we were doing. I stood on a projecting rock waving my hat to gain his attention, for my voice was drowned by the roaring of the falls, when just at that moment I saw him take his knife from its sheath and step forward to cut the line. He had evidently decided that it was better to go over with his boat as it was, than to wait for her to be broken to pieces. As he leaned over, the boat sheered again into the stream, the stern-post broke away, and she was loose. With perfect composure Bradley seized the great scull oar, placed it in the stern rowlock, and pulled with all his power—and he was a strong fellow—to turn the bow of the boat down stream, for he wished to go bow down rather than to drift broadside on. One, two strokes were made, a third just as she went over, and the boat was fairly turned; she went down almost beyond our sight, though we were more than a hundred feet above the river. Then she came up again on a great wave, and down and up, then around behind some great rocks, and was lost in the tumultuous foam below.

We stood speechless with fear; we saw no boat; Bradley was gone. But now, away below, we saw something coming out of the waves. It was evidently a boat; a moment more and we saw Bradley standing on deck swinging his hat to show that he was all right. But he was in a whirlpool. The stern-post of his boat remained attached to the line which was in our possession. How badly she was disabled we knew not. I directed Sumner and Powell to run along the cliff and see if they could reach him from below. Rhodes, Hall, and myself ran to the other boat, jumped aboard, pushed out, and away we went over the falls. A wave rolled over us and our craft became unmanageable; another great wave struck us, the boat rolled over, and tumbled, and tossed, I know not how. All I know is, that Bradley was soon picking us up. Before long we had all right again, and rowed to the cliff and waited until Sumner and Powell came up. After a difficult climb they reached us, when we ran two or three miles farther, and turned again to the north-west, continuing until night, when we ran out of the granite once more.

At twelve o'clock on August 29th we emerged from the Grand Cañon of the Colorado, and entered a valley from which low mountains were seen coming to the river below. We recognized this as the Grand Wash.

A few years before, a party of Mormons taking with them a boat, set out from St. George in Utah, and came down to the mouth of the Grand Wash, where they divided, a portion of the party crossing the river to explore the San Francisco Mountains. Three men, Hamblin, Miller, and Crosby, taking the boat, went on down the river to Colville, landing a few miles below the mouth of the Rio Virgen. We had their manuscript journal with us, so we knew the stream well enough.

At night we camped on the left bank in a mesquite thicket. The sense of relief from danger and the joy of success were great. When he who has been chained by wounds to a hospital cot until his canvas tent seems like a dungeon, and the groans of those who lie about him are an increasing torture—when such a prisoner at last goes out into the open field, what a world he sees! How beautiful the sky, how bright the sunshine, what "floods of delicious music" pour from the throats of the birds, how sweet the fragrance of earth, and tree, and blossom! The first hour of convalescent freedom seems rich recompense for all the pain, the gloom and the terror.

Something like this was the feeling we experienced that night. Ever before us had been an unknown danger heavier than any immediate peril. Every waking hour passed in the Grand Cañon had been one of toil. We had watched with deep solicitude the steady disappearance of our scant supply of rations, and from time to time when we were hungry had seen the river snatch a portion of the little left. Danger and toil were endured in those gloomy depths where often the clouds hid the sky by day, and but a narrow zone of stars could be seen at night. Only during the few hours of deep sleep consequent on hard labor had the roar of the mad waters been hushed; now the danger was over, the toil had ceased, the gloom had disappeared, and the firmament was bounded only by the wide horizon.

The river rolled by in silent majesty; the quiet of the camp was sweet, our joy was almost ecstasy. We sat till long after midnight talking of the Grand Cañon, of home, and, more than all, of the three men who had left us. Were they wandering in those depths, unable to find a way out? Were they searching over the desert lands above for water? Or were they nearing the settlements with the same feeling of relief that we ourselves experienced?

We ran through two or three short, low cañons the next day, and on emerging from one, discovered a band of Indians in the valley below. They saw us and scampered away to hide among the rocks. Although we stopped and called for them to return, not an Indian could be seen.

Two or three miles farther down, in turning a short bend in the river, we came upon

OUR MESSENGER'S WIFE.

another camp. So near were we before they could see us that I could shout to them, and being able to speak a little of their language, I told them we were friends. But they all fled to the rocks except a man, a woman, and two children. We stopped and talked with them. They were without lodges, but had built little shelters of boughs, under which they wallowed in the sand. The man's only garment was a hat, the woman's a string of beads. At first they were evidently much terrified, but when I talked to them in their own language, told them we were friends, and inquired after people in the Mormon towns, they were soon reassured, and begged for tobacco. Of this precious article we had none to spare. Sumner looked in the boat for something to give them, and found a little piece of colored soap, which they received as a valuable present; rather, however, as a thing of beauty than of use. They were either unwilling or unable to tell us anything about other Indians or white people, so we pushed off, for we had no time to lose.

Soon after dinner one of the men exclaimed: "Yonder's an Indian in the river!" Looking for a few minutes, we certainly did see two or three figures. The men bent to their oars and pulled toward them. Approaching, we saw three white men and an Indian hauling a seine. We were at the mouth of the long-sought river!

As we came near, the men seemed far less surprised to see us than we were to see them. They evidently knew who we were, and on talking with them they told us that we had been reported lost long ago, and that some months before a messenger had been sent from Salt Lake City with instructions for them to watch for any fragments or relics of our party that might drift down the stream.

Our new-found friends, Mr. Asa and his two sons, told me they were the pioneers of a town that was to be built on the bank.

Eighteen or twenty miles up the valley of the Rio Virgen there were two Mormon towns, St. Joseph and St. Thomas, and we dispatched an Indian to the latter place to bring any letters that might be there for us.

Our arrival here was very opportune in consideration of the state of our supplies. We had only about ten pounds of flour, and fifteen pounds of dried apples, though there was still left seventy or eighty pounds of coffee.

The next afternoon the Indian returned with a letter informing us that Bishop Leithead, of St. Thomas, and two or three other Mormons were coming down with a wagon of supplies for us. They arrived about sundown. Mr. Asa treated us with great kindness. Bishop Leithead brought in his wagon two or three dozen melons and many other little luxuries, and we were comfortable once more.

The next morning, September 1st, Sumner, Bradley, Hawkins, and Hall, taking on a small supply of rations, started down the Colorado with the boats. It was their intention to go to Fort Mojave, and, perhaps, from thence overland to Los Angelos. Captain Powell and myself returned with Bishop Leithead to St. Thomas, and proceeded thence to Salt Lake City.

The exploration of the Great Cañon of the Colorado was accomplished.

Lower Cañon of the Kanab. (3,000 feet deep.)

EPILOGUE

JOHN Wesley Powell went on to further explore the canyon country of the Southwest, and to communicate his findings to an interested American public. See, for instance, *An Overland Trip to the Grand Canyon* in which he describes his 1870 search through Utah and Arizona for his lost men, the ones who had left his party in the depths of Grand Canyon when further downstream travel seemed to them impossible. He learned their fate — killed by Indians after climbing out of the canyon. A plaque, below, now commemorates their role in history.

Plaque on the eastern side of Separation Canyon, marking the place where the Howland brothers and William H. Dunn left the 1869 Powell expedition.